CULTURE SMART!

CUBA

Mandy Macdonald and
Russell Maddicks

·K·U·P·E·R·A·R·D·

This book is available for special discounts for bulk purchases for sales promotions or premiums. Special editions, including personalized covers, excerpts of existing books, and corporate imprints, can be created in large quantities for special needs.

For more information contact Kuperard publishers at the address below.

ISBN 978 1 85733 848 5
This book is also available as an e-book: eISBN 978 1 85733 846 1

British Library Cataloguing in Publication Data
A CIP catalogue entry for this book is available from the British Library

First published in Great Britain
by Kuperard, an imprint of Bravo Ltd
59 Hutton Grove, London N12 8DS
Tel: +44 (0) 20 8446 2440 Fax: +44 (0) 20 8446 2441
www.culturesmart.co.uk
Inquiries: sales@kuperard.co.uk

Series Editor Geoffrey Chesler
Design Bobby Birchall

Printed in Malaysia

Cover image: *Street scene with vintage American car in downtown Havana.* © iStock.

Images on the following pages reproduced under Creative Commons Attribution-Share Alike 4.0 International license: 13 (bottom), 63 (bottom) © Velvet; 39 © Max.dai.yang; 74, 104 (middle) © Ji-Elle ; 88 © Jakub Szypulka; 97, 103 © Arnoud Joris Maaswinkel; 100 © Susanne Bollinger; 106 © Stephan Braun, Latin-Mag; 123 © Happypepe; 132 (bottom) © Gotanero.

Reproduced under Creative Commons Attribution-Share Alike 3.0 Unported license: 13 (top) © Anagoria; 21 (bottom) © Collectie Stichting Nationaal Museum van Wereldculturen; 34 © photo by Radomil, 6 June 2005, Poznań; 41 © Nigel Pacquette; 45 © Henryk Kotowski; 57, 132 (top) © Photo by Adam Jones adamjones.freeservers.com; 66, 91, 101 (top), 158 © Jorge Royan; 71 © Bin im Garten; 72 © Leon Petrosyan; 77 © Eggenbergurbock23; 89 © Dominique Michel; 90 © Maxim Nedashkovskiy; 95 © takethemud; 101 (bottom) © BitBoy (Flickr user); 108 © XIIIfromTOKYO; 109 © Lucash; 110 © Bgabel; 116 © ZTC; 118 © BluesyPete; 119, 139 © Mmoyaq; 121 (top) © Rainer Jung; 125 © Jezhotwells; 126 © Escla; 130 © Mariordo; 131 © LukaszKatlewa; 143 © Cubadebate.

Under Creative Commons Attribution-Share Alike 3.0 Germany license: 35 © Koard, Peter, German Federal Archives.

Creative Commons Attribution-Share Alike 2.5 Generic license: 19 (bottom) © Michal Zalewski.

Creative Commons Attribution-Share Alike 2.0 Generic license: 14 © Laura Gooch; 21 (top) © Glogg, Peter, Switzerland; 23 © Emmanuel Huybrechts from Laval, Canada; 49, 51 © Matias Garabedian from Montreal, Canada; 79, 117 © Christopher Michel; 107 (top) © Mike Fleming from London, England; 107 (bottom) © Lopsterx; 111 © dalbera from Paris, France; 112 © Gerry Zambonini; 115 © Roger DeWitt from Same, USA.

About the Author

MANDY MACDONALD is an Australian writer, researcher, and translator living in Scotland. A graduate of Sydney and Cambridge Universities, she specializes in international affairs with an emphasis on Latin American development issues and gender equality. Mandy has worked in Cuba and has written many articles, papers, and books on Cuba and Central America. She is also the author of *Culture Smart! Belgium* (2005) and *Simple Guides: Greek Philosophy* (2009).

RUSSELL MADDICKS is a BBC-trained journalist, translator, and travel writer. A graduate in Economic and Social History from the University of Hull, he has spent twenty years living and working in South and Central America, most recently as Regional Specialist for BBC Monitoring. A fluent Spanish speaker, he has made many extended trips to Cuba. He is the author of the *Bradt Guide to Venezuela* (2011), *Culture Smart! Venezuela* (2012), and the award-winning *Culture Smart! Ecuador* (2014).

The Culture Smart! series is continuing to expand.
For further information and latest titles visit
www.culturesmart.co.uk

The publishers would like to thank **CultureSmart!**Consulting for its help in researching and developing the concept for this series.

contents

Map of Cuba 7
Introduction 8
Key Facts 10

Chapter 1: LAND AND PEOPLE 12
• Geographical Snapshot 12
• Climate 14
• A Brief History 16
• The Political System 39
• The Economy 43
• Looking Ahead: Obama's Big Thaw and the Future of US–Cuba Relations 47

Chapter 2: VALUES AND ATTITUDES 48
• Resilience and Resourcefulness 49
• The Spirit of the Revolution 50
• Dissent 52
• Attitudes Toward Race 54
• Attitudes Toward Religion 55
• Men and Women 57
• LGBT Cubans Come Out of the Cold War Closet 58
• Attitudes Toward Foreigners 60

Chapter 3: CUSTOMS AND TRADITIONS 62
• Catholic Traditions 62
• Afro-Cuban Traditions 65
• Celebrating History 67
• Cultural Events 68
• Public Holidays 70
• Carnivals 70
• Secular Wedding Palaces 73
• Sweet Fifteen 74

Chapter 4: MAKING FRIENDS 76
• Meeting People 77
• What to Wear 79

- Conversation Starters and Stoppers 80
- Breaking Out of the Tourist Bubble 83
- Staying Longer 85

Chapter 5: THE CUBANS AT HOME 86
- Quality of Life 86
- Town and Country 88
- Housing 90
- Health Care 92
- Education 94
- The Changing Family 95
- The Daily Round 96
- In the Community 98
- The CDRS 99

Chapter 6: TIME OUT 100
- Food 101
- *Comida Criolla*: Popular Cuban Dishes 103
- Drinks 105
- Cocktails With History 106
- The Arts 107
- Sports and Outdoor Activities 114
- Shopping for Pleasure 116
- Cuban Cigars 116
- Places to Visit 117

Chapter 7: TRAVEL, HEALTH, AND SAFETY 122
- Getting Around 122
- In Towns and Resorts 130
- Where to Stay 132
- Health 134
- Crime and Safety 136

Chapter 8: BUSINESS BRIEFING 138
- The Economic Climate 138
- Cuba as a Business Partner 140
- Government and Business 141

contents

- The Legal Framework 141
- The Workforce 142
- Unions 143
- The Importance of Personal Relationships 144
- Be Prepared 145
- Making a Proposal 146
- Meetings 146
- Negotiating 147
- Decision Making and Follow-Up 148
- Contracts 149
- Resolving Disputes 149

Chapter 9: COMMUNICATING 150

- Language 150
- Written Communication 152
- Forms of Address 153
- Direct Interaction 154
- Humor 155
- The Media 156
- Telephone 159
- Internet 161
- Mail 162
- Conclusion 163

Further Reading 165
Index 166
Acknowledgments 168

Map of Cuba

GULF OF MEXICO
U.S.A.
Straits of Florida
THE BAHAMAS
La Habana (Havana)
Mariel
Matanzas
Varadero
CORDILLERA DE GUANIGUANICO
Suridero de Batabano
Santa Clara
Cienfuegos
Remedios
Sancti Spiritus
Morón
Ciego de Avila
Trinidad
Pinar del Río
ISLA DE LA JUVENTUD
Bay of Pigs
Yucatán Channel
Camagüey
Las Tunas
Holguín
Bayamo
Manzanillo
Baracoa
SIERRA MAESTRA
Santiago de Cuba
Guantánamo
CAYMAN ISLANDS (UK)
CARIBBEAN SEA
JAMAICA
Jamaica Channel

introduction

The largest island in the Caribbean and a popular, sun-drenched mecca for snowbirds from Canada and Europe, Cuba is an anomaly: a country that buzzes with Latin American life, sensual music, and abundant positivity, but also feels stuck in a timeless torpor, where the resilience and make-and-mend ingenuity of the Cuban people are constantly put to the test.

For more than fifty years Cuba has been seen almost exclusively through the prism of the Cuban Revolution, and the ensuing hot and cold standoff with the United States, its superpower neighbor to the north. At its most extreme point, during the Cuban missile crisis, this power play between the US and socialist Cuba, and its backers in the Soviet Union, brought the world to the brink of nuclear destruction.

The classic American cars—some more rust than metal—that chug past the crumbling seafront mansions of Havana, and the long lines outside state-owned stores for rationed goods, are a daily reminder of the US trade embargo that continues to limit access to consumer goods and investment capital. However, with the historic thaw in relations brokered by US President Barack Obama and Cuban leader Raúl Castro in 2015 there is a sense that real change is coming to Cuba, a hope that the embargo will be lifted or significantly eased, that the restrictions on US tourists will be completely removed, and Cubans will be afforded greater freedom to travel and to set up businesses.

Alongside the hopes there are fears: that Cuba's exemplary health care and education systems may be diluted, and rationing phased out, effectively widening the gap between those Cubans who have access to foreign currency and the majority who struggle to get by on state salaries and pensions.

Fidel Castro may have left office in 2008, to be succeeded by his brother Raúl, but after half a century in power his shadow still hangs over the country. Cuba's tropical brand of Communism was Fidel's own personal experiment, and Cubans are still living with the consequences of standing up to the USA and taking such a prominent role on the world stage.

In this book you will find chapters on the history and deeply held values that make Cuba the unique mixture of cultural vibrancy and political intransigence it is today. We look at what everyday life is like for Cubans, how they get by in a state-run system, how you can meet Cubans outside the usual tourist traps, and what it's like to do business in a centrally run economy. Thoroughly revised and updated, *Culture Smart! Cuba* aims to give visitors a better understanding of the infinitely resourceful Cuban people, who despite severe hardships and shortages over many years remain ever-optimistic and fiercely proud of their heritage and culture.

Key Facts

Official Name	República de Cuba	A member of WTO, ECLAC, OAS, ALBA, UNCTAD, ACP
Capital City	Havana (La Habana)	Pop. 2.1 million (2015 est.)
Main Cities	Santiago de Cuba (426,0000), Camagüey (305,000),	Holguín (277,000), Trinidad (45,000)
Area	42,426 sq. miles (109,884 sq. km)	Largest island in the Caribbean
Climate	Tropical, with dry season December to April/May. Rainy season June to November	Average highs of 90°F (32°C) in July/ August. Lows of 70°F (21°C) in January
Population	11.2 million (2015 est.)	
Ethnic Makeup	In 1990, 51% mulatto (mixed-race Spanish/African), 37% white, 11% black, 1% Chinese	
Languages	Spanish	Some English in tourist areas
Religion	Largest Christian group is Roman Catholic, plus minority Protestants, Evangelicals, Jehovah's Witnesses, and Quakers. There is a small Jewish community. The animistic Yoruba religion known in Cuba as Santería, or Regla de Ochá, is widely practiced.	
Government	One-party state ruled by the Communist Party of Cuba (PCC). Elections to the National Assembly are held every five years.	The President is also Chief of State, Head of Government, First Secretary of the PCC, and Commander-in-Chief.

Currency	Two-currency system: Cuban Peso (CUP) used by locals. Convertible Peso (CUC) used by tourists pegged around 1–1 with US dollar	Neither can be exchanged outside Cuba. Surcharge on US dollar exchange. No surcharge on euros or Canadian dollars
GDP Per Capita	US $ 6,789 (2013 est.)	
Media	Daily newspapers: *Granma*, *Juventud Rebelde*, *Trabajadores*. Several weeklies and magazines	Five TV channels; seven national radio stations. All media are state-controlled.
Media: English-language	*Granma International*, weekly published online in English and several other languages. *Cartelera*, bilingual cultural weekly	
Electricity	110 volts, 60 Hz	European appliances need 2-pin flat or round adaptors.
Video/TV	NTSC – DVD Zone 4	
Internet Domain	.cu	
Telephone	The country code is 53. City codes: Havana 7, Santiago 226, Camagüey 32, Holguín 24, Trinidad 41	For direct-dialed calls out of Cuba, dial 119. Numbers often change. Some calls are still made by operator.
Time Zone	Standard time is 5 hours behind UTC/ GMT.	Daylight saving time, March to October: GMT –4

chapter one

LAND & PEOPLE

GEOGRAPHICAL SNAPSHOT

Cubans like to say that their long, slim island lies in the turquoise waters of the Caribbean like a sleeping crocodile. Located at the mouth of the Gulf of Mexico, Cuba is about 97 miles (156 km) south of Florida, 130 miles (210 km) east of Mexico, and 87 miles (140 km) north of Jamaica. The largest island of the Greater Antilles, it is actually part of an archipelago that includes the small Isla de la Juventud (Isle of Youth) off the southwest coast, and about 1,600 coastal islets, keys, and coral reefs.

The mainland stretches some 776 miles (1,250 km) from Baracoa and Guantánamo in the south to Havana and Pinar del Río in the north, and is only 119 miles (191 km) at its widest point. Slightly smaller than England, and about the same size as the US state of Virginia, the total surface area of the island is 42,805 sq. miles (110,861 sq. km).

Cuba is largely low-lying, with a fringe of white sandy beaches, leading inland to a flat or gently undulating landscape of tobacco farms, sugar plantations, wetlands, and forested hills. The three main mountain ranges are the eastern Sierra Maestra, which contains Cuba's highest peak, Pico Turquino (6,476 ft/1,974 m), the Sierra del Escambray in central Cuba, and the Cordillera de Guaniguanico in the

west. The landscape around the tobacco growing valleys of Viñales is characterized by *mogotes*, isolated domes and ridges of forested limestone that rear up straight out of the grassy plains. Only a few rivers are navigable. About 4 percent of the main island is wetlands; the most important is the Zapata Swamp, in the southwest, an important nature reserve.

A falling population, reforestation programs, the lack of large-scale industrial farming or timber extraction, and good park management have left

Cuba's wilderness areas and reefs in fairly good shape compared to its Caribbean neighbors. About 14 percent of Cuba's landmass is protected in national and local reserves, including fourteen national parks. Six protected areas are designated as UNESCO biosphere reserves, including Cuchillas del Toa near Baracoa in the eastern province of

Guantánamo (which includes Cuba's longest river, the Río de Miel), and the 80,060-acre (32,400-hectare) Parque Baconoa, the largest reserve, near Santiago de Cuba. The Humboldt National Park in the Nipe-Sagua-Baracoa Mountains on the north coast of eastern Cuba, has been designated a UNESCO natural heritage site and is considered one of the most biologically diverse tropical island sites on earth.

Cuba has fourteen provinces, including the capital, plus a special municipality, the Isle of Youth. About one-fifth of the population of 11.2 million lives in Havana.

CLIMATE

Cuba has a tropical climate with a dry season from December to April/May and a rainy season from June to November. Temperatures can reach a sweltering 90°F (32°C) in July, August, and September, the hottest months, and dip to a balmy 79°F (26°C)

in January, the coolest month. Santiago de Cuba is generally hotter than Havana by a few degrees, and inland daytime temperatures in eastern Cuba, where there is no sea breeze to offer relief from the searing tropical heat, can rise to around 97° F (36° C) in July and August.

February and March are the driest months and October, during the hurricane season, is the wettest month. Average annual rainfall is around 52 inches (1,320 mm), the highest rainfalls occurring in the mountains and the lowest along the coast and on the islands. At any time of year, the weather can switch from glorious sunshine to a torrential downpour and back to sunshine again in an hour or two. As the wet season begins, temperature and humidity rise together, and the beach becomes a place of refuge, with sea temperatures topping 77° F (25° C), alleviated by the breeze.

Hurricane Prone

Hurricanes are most frequent from August to November, during the wet season. Cuba lies along the main hurricane path through the Caribbean and is affected by a major storm every three years or so, with a serious direct hit every eight or nine years. The most devastating hurricanes in recent years were Gustav and Ike, which hit the island just ten days apart in 2008, causing US $9.7bn of damage and leveling 82,000 homes in the province of Pinar del Río. Hurricane Sandy struck eastern Cuba in October 2012, destroying 17,000 homes and damaging 150,000 before going on to hit the Eastern Seaboard of the US.

Few people died in these hurricanes as Cuba has a well-rehearsed civil and military response, including evacuation of threatened communities and storm shelters. Emergency procedures are posted in all hotels and in other public places, and broadcast on radio and TV. All modern housing and hotels are built to withstand hurricanes, and older hotels have been reinforced.

A BRIEF HISTORY

Like many of its neighbors, the history of Cuba is one of hardship and foreign intervention, including the brutal conquest by Spain of the indigenous people that left few survivors, the transhipment of a million African slaves to work on huge and highly profitable sugar cane plantations, and then a long fight for independence from Spanish rule that only ended in 1898 when the US military got involved. Cuba also shook off the yolk of the US-supported dictator Fulgencio Batista in 1959, only to shape its own course under the socialist direction of Fidel Castro, who nationalized American companies, leading to a trade embargo by the US that has endured for more than fifty years. Cuba's subsequent decision to accept the protection of the Soviet Union following the botched US attempt to topple the new regime with the Bay of Pigs invasion of April 17, 1961, drew it into a wider Cold War power game that led directly to the 1962 Cuban Missile Crisis and a hardening of US attitudes.

When the Soviet Union collapsed in 1989, Cuba was forced to make do on its own in what came to be known as the Special Period. A time of extreme hardship, rationing, and migration, it forced a complete rethink of the Cuban economy and a new focus on tourism and culture to supplement failing sugar profits.

Since Fidel Castro stepped down as president for health reasons in 2008, his younger brother Raúl has introduced limited but important reforms, allowing Cubans to open private businesses like *paladares* (small restaurants) and *casas particulares* (guesthouses), and to buy and sell houses. Negotiations with President Barack Obama, brokered by the Catholic Church, have also resulted in the reopening of the US Embassy in Havana and a partial easing of US restrictions on trade and travel, although the embargo will remain in place until the US Congress votes to remove it.

Origins and Conquest

Few modern archaeological studies have been done in Cuba and the origins of human settlement are unclear. The first inhabitants, sometimes referred to as the Guanajatabeyes, are believed to have migrated from the South American mainland and survived from hunting and fishing along the coast of Cuba, possibly arriving as early 2,500 BCE. They were later pushed to the western end of the island by the much later arrival of two Arawak groups, the Siboney and the Taíno, who also came from the area around present-day Venezuela and brought a more sophisticated material culture based on agriculture. These were the people Christopher Columbus met in October 1492 on his first voyage to the Americas.

Columbus waxed lyrical about the lush vegetation and handsome natives, but he found negligible amounts of gold or pearls in Cuba in 1492 or his subsequent trip in 1494, so it was not until 1510, under Diego Velázquez de Cuéllar, that the Spanish conquest began in earnest.

CUBA—WHAT'S IN A NAME?

"This is the most beautiful land that human eyes have ever seen," wrote Christopher Columbus after landing on the coast of present-day Holguin in eastern Cuba on October 28, 1492. The Admiral of the Ocean Sea had voyaged from Spain to find a sea route to the riches of "Cipangu" (Japan) and Cathay (China) and was anxious to meet the great ruler Kublai Khan. Rather than palaces of gold all he found were two abandoned fisherman's huts and later some large communal houses where he described men and women with "the herbs for smoking which they are in a habit of using," the first written record of tobacco smoking. The name the natives used for the rolls of burning leaves they inhaled? *Cohíbas.*

The first name Columbus gave to the isand was Juana, in tribute to Queen Isabela's son Don Juan, the Prince of Asturias. The native Taínos told him their island was called *Cubanacan* or *Coabana* (meaning, great place), and *Colba*, *Cubao*, and *Cuba* (meaning, where fertile land is abundant), but Cuba is the one that stuck.

Velázquez de Cuéllar arrived on an expedition from Hispaniola, founding the first Spanish settlement in Baracoa and claiming the island for the Spanish Crown and the Roman Catholic faith.

Bartolomé de las Casas, however, the Spanish priest who recorded the eradication of the native peoples with horror in his *History of the Indies*, described the violent conquest of the Indians as "far . . . from the purpose of God and His Church." The conquered Siboney and Taíno were coerced into labor on the

lands they had lost, and by 1515 most of the main cities and towns of modern-day Cuba had been founded.

The indigenous *cacique* (chieftain) Hatuey came from Hispaniola to warn the Taínos of the fate that awaited them at the hands of the Spanish and led a brief insurrection against the conquistadors that ended in 1512 when he was captured and burned at the stake. Asked if he would convert before burning, the proud *cacique* replied: "If Spaniards go to heaven, I prefer to go to hell." Today, he is considered Cuba's first rebel and included in the pantheon of revolutionary heros. A popular brand of beer is named after him.

By the mid-sixteenth century most of the Taínos had either been killed or had melted away into the mountains. Recent investigations suggest Taíno populations held out for many generations in the eastern part of the island around Baracoa.

Plunder and Piracy

In the sixteenth and seventeenth centuries Cuba's location at the gateway to the Gulf of Mexico made it an important staging post for conquest, trade, and defense against French, Dutch, and English privateers. The large port of Havana quickly became a key rendezvous point for all the treasure-laden ships coming from Veracruz, Cartagena, and Portobello, before they set sail in flotilla to the Canary Islands and then Seville.

From Cuba, the Spanish exported fine woods, leather, citrus fruits, tobacco, and sugar, which was grown by slave labor on large plantations. The first evidence of African slaves in Cuba dates from 1513, and by the seventeenth century the slave trade was well established, with over a million slaves brought to the island. This increasingly lively commerce, together with constant military activity in the seas around the Americas, attracted the attention of pirates and privateers, who did much damage to coastal towns. Havana was sacked by the French pirate Jacques de Sores in 1555, prompting the building of impressive fortifications that dissuaded Francis Drake from doing the same in 1587.

A Brief British Occupation

In 1762 a large British armed fleet captured Havana, as part of a British offensive against Spain at the end of the Seven Years' War (1756–63). The British invaders immediately opened up trade between Cuba and Britain and its North American possessions. Within a year, however, Cuba and the Philippines were returned to the Spanish in exchange for Florida, by the Treaty of Paris in 1763. Unfortunately, the most lasting effect was a sharp escalation in the slave trade with Africa.

Sugar Rush

As the demand for sugar in Europe and North America soared, Cuba stepped up production and by 1827 it was the world's major producer. Sugar was to remain Cuba's principal export for nearly two hundred years, but production required massive slave labor. As slavery ended in Santo Domingo (today's Dominican Republic) in 1791 and Haiti in 1803, exiled slave owners flocked to eastern Cuba. The advent of steam power and railways in the mid-nineteenth century accelerated production and profit but made life even harsher for the slaves and other workers.

The early nineteenth century saw many Latin American countries win independence from Spain, but not Cuba—the profits from Cuba were too great. *Criollo* (creole) planters, born in Cuba of Spanish origin, resented the colonial power, wanting property rights and the right to develop their own capital. The mid-century emigration of poor Spaniards to Cuba and growing trade with the United States made this call both louder and more rational. But Spain clung fiercely to its cash cow, and it was not until 1878 that it conceded even promises of reform and autonomy.

AN ANTHEM BORN IN BATTLE

Cuba's National Anthem *La Bayamesa* dates back to the Ten Years' War when the rebel forces of Carlos Manuel de Céspedes seized the city of Bayamo from Spanish imperial control on October 10, 1868. The song, penned by Perucho Figueredo, is a rousing call to action that echoes the sentiments of the revolutionary slogan seen all over Cuba: *Patria o Muerte*! (Homeland or Death!)

¡Al combate, corred, Bayameses!,
Que la patria os contempla orgullosa;
No temáis una muerte gloriosa,
Que morir por la patria es vivir.

Run to battle, men of Bayamo!
The motherland looks proudly to you;
Do not fear a glorious death,
Because to die for the motherland is to live.

Three Wars of Independence from Spain

The Ten Years' War (1868–78) was ignited when, in October 1868, Manuel de Céspedes, a *criollo* planter, freed all the slaves on his small plantation at La Demajagua and called for independence from Spain in a speech known to every Cuban as *el Grito de Yara* (the Cry of Yara). Thousands of freed slaves, peasants, and indentured laborers flocked to Céspedes' rebel army, led in the field by Máximo Gómez and Antonio Maceo. As the Spanish brought in more and more soldiers, the rebels, calling themselves *mambises*, after Juan Mambí, a Dominican freedom fighter, turned successfully to guerrilla warfare.

After Céspedes' death in 1874, a stalemate in 1878 led to the Pact of Zanjón, whereby the landowners and the Spanish agreed on some reforms, but it was swiftly followed by the unsuccesful uprising known as the Little War, in 1879–80. Although slavery was finally abolished in 1886, insurrection smoldered on.

In 1894 Spain cancelled a trade agreement between the US and Cuba, precipitating the Cuban

JOSÉ MARTÍ, NATIONAL HERO

Born in Havana in 1853, José Martí was a journalist, poet, and writer, and one of Latin America's great literary figures. He was also a political activist who argued strongly for racial equality, and, as an exile in the United States, mobilized support for independence among other Cuban exiles. He was also the first to warn of the danger the US represented to Cuba, as US companies moved into the Cuban sugar industry following the end of slavery. But it was his death in the Cuban War of Independence on 19 May, 1895—just one month after landing again on Cuban soil—that immortalized him as a national hero.

Martí's image appears everywhere in Cuba, both outside and inside schools, hospitals, and government offices, and on the one-peso note. The most popular Cuban song of all time, "Guantanamera," includes lines from Martí's poetry collection *Versos Sencillos*:

Yo soy un hombre sincero
De donde crece la palma,
Y antes de morirme quiero
Echar mis versos del alma.

I am a sincere man,
From where the palm trees grow,
And before I die, I want to
Pour out the verses from my soul.

War of Independence in 1895. The rebels sabotaged the sugar industry and Spanish property, and Spain retaliated by driving the rural population into concentration camps, where thousands died. The rebellion was led again by Gómez and Maceo, under the political inspiration of José Martí (see box). In 1897 Spain offered Cuba autonomy, but the rebels insisted on full independence.

The final chapter was played out in the brief Spanish–American War (1898), which erupted when an American battleship, USS *Maine*, blew up in mysterious circumstances in Havana harbor on February 15. Congress declared war on Spain on April 21; US forces won swift victories in eastern Cuba, and a treaty was signed in April 1899 giving Cuba, Puerto Rico, Guam, and the Philippines to the US.

The Pseudo-Republic

The defeat of Spain did not mean independence for Cuba, however. Cuba became nominally independent in 1902 under its first president, Tomás Estrada Palma, but Spanish rule was effectively replaced by the de facto rule of the US under the Platt Amendment, which gave the US the power to intervene at any time "for the preservation of Cuban independence [and] the maintenance of a government adequate for the protection of life, property and individual liberty." The US intervened four times in Cuba before the repeal of the agreement in 1934.

GUANTÁNAMO BAY

The most controversial element of the Platt Amendment was the agreement signed in 1903 between the two governments to lease Guantánamo Bay to the USA. The 45 square miles of territory have been used as a naval base, currently the oldest US overseas naval base in the world, and since 2002 to house prisoners from the US war in Afghanistan, Iraq, and elsewhere, in a kind of legal limbo. Cuba has consistently called for the return of Guantánamo since the 1959 Revolution, arguing that the lease was forced on the Cuban government, is illegal under international law, and the naval base sits on territory "usurped" by US Marines in 1898.

For over fifty years Cuba has refused to cash the US $4,085 cheque sent by the US each year to lease the land, and in September 2015, following a meeting with President Barack Obama, Raúl Castro reiterated Cuba's insistence that full normalization of relations will require an end to the US trade embargo and the return of Guantánamo.

The Big US Sugar Boom

With most of its population poor, illiterate, and in ill health after years of war, Cuba was utterly dependent on the United States, which made no more effort to develop it than Spain had done. The sugar industry was modernized and mechanized but became a monopoly serving only the interests of the United States, the main market for Cuban sugar and the main investor in the industry.

By the mid-1920s, US companies controlled two-thirds of Cuban agriculture. The sugar boom of the

1920s paid for imposing public buildings and luxurious houses for the wealthy but gave nothing to the poor. US companies built roads and railways and installed banks, electricity, and the world's first automated telephone system, but repatriated all the profits.

The Cuban government had little political power or authority. Corruption bloomed, particularly under General Gerardo Machado (1925–33), while opposition from the labor movement and the political left was mercilessly repressed. Influenced by the ideas and propagandists of the Russian Revolution, the Cuban Communist Party was founded in 1925 and became strong in the labor movement.

Into this society Fidel Alejandro Castro Ruz was born on August 13, 1926, in the rural hamlet of Birán in the eastern province of Holguín. The illegitimate son of wealthy plantation owner Ángel María Bautista Castro y Argiz, and his maid Lina Ruz Gonzalez, the young Fidel experienced firsthand the hard lives of the rural poor working the cane fields.

The Rise of Batista

In 1933 massive opposition to Machado's government culminated in a general strike, and Machado fled into exile. Into the ensuing political confusion, which included a progressive but extremely short-lived government headed by Ramón Grau San Martín and Antonio Guiteras, stepped Fulgencio Batista, a young mulatto army officer, who seized power in January 1934.

Batista was to retain his power and influence in one way or another for the next fifteen years, supported by both the US government and the Mafia. In 1940, he brought in a new constitution that promoted labor rights, a minimum wage, and even equal pay for equal work, and cooperated with the Communist Party when he found it expedient. Losing the 1944 elections, he withdrew to Florida, leaving Cuba practically ungovernable. Returning in 1952 just before the presidential elections, he carried out a bloodless coup, beginning a violent, crime-ridden, seven-year dictatorship.

These were the years when the Tropicana Club, with its voluptuous dancers, was described as the largest and most beautiful night club in the world, plush casinos were run by mob bosses like Santo "Louie Santos" Trafficante Jr., and Meyer Lansky, and Hollywood royalty like Errol Flynn and Marlene Dietrich rubbed shoulders with Frank Sinatra and Ava Gardner at the Nacional Hotel.

At the same, the corpses appearing daily on the streets of Cuba's main towns, bore gruesome witness to the price of opposition.

From Moncada to the Sierra Maestra

The Cuban Revolution made its first serious mark with the rebel attack on the Moncada barracks in Santiago de Cuba on July 26, 1953.

Fidel Castro had already begun building a movement to overthrow Batista, principally among radicals in the left-wing Ortodoxo Party, formed in 1947, to which he belonged at the time. The capture of the Moncada barracks, the country's second-most important garrison, was intended

to set off a popular uprising throughout the country. But the rebels were outnumbered and soon overpowered. Many were tortured to death, and Castro and twenty-eight others were imprisoned. Released in May 1955 in an amnesty, the rebels promptly resumed their struggle under a new organization, the 26 July Movement.

Before long, Fidel left for Mexico to plan his campaign, as Martí had done, from exile. There he met the young Argentinian doctor Ernesto Guevara, known to his friends—and now to the world—as "Che" (the Argentinian slang for "buddy").

On November 25, 1956, after months of planning and fund-raising, eighty-two revolutionaries embarked for Cuba in bad weather in an old, leaky motorboat, the *Granma*. Running aground in dense mangrove swamps, they were immediately decimated by Batista's troops. Just twelve of them reached the Sierra Maestra, from where they slowly gained the trust and support of the local peasants, built up a guerrilla army, and began to win clashes with Batista's troops. The

BOAT THAT LAUNCHED A REVOLUTION, A NEWSPAPER, AND A PROVINCE

Visitors often wonder why the official newspaper of the Central Committee of the Communist Party is called *Granma*. Is it the name of a revolutionary hero? The acronym of a clandestine group? A word in Russian like Pravda? Well, none of the above is the answer. The name comes from the 60-foot (18 m), 12-person cabin cruiser that on November 25, 1956, took Fidel Castro, his brother Raúl, Che Guevara, and the seventy-nine revolutionaries who accompanied them, on a turbulent, leaky, seven-day voyage through rough seas from Tuxpan in Veracruz, Mexico, to Playa Las Coloradas on the southern end of Cuba, where they began the fight against the Batista regime. The fighting was so fierce that of the original eighty-two fewer than twenty made it to the Sierra Maestra mountains where Fidel Castro regrouped his troops. This "Granma Group", as it became known, would form the inner core of the Cuban Revolution in war and later in peace.

Built in 1943, and named in affectionate tribute to the original owner's grandma, the boat was purchased by the young revolutionaries for US $15,000. It is now housed behind glass in its own mini-museum in front of the Museum of the Revolution in Havana. The area where it made its landing is now named Granma Province, and the Landing of the Granma National Park (Parque Nacional Desembarco del Granma), set up to preserve the marine terraces and impressive cliffs along the coast, was declared a UNESCO World Heritage Site in 1999. Not bad for a little boat.

Sierra was also a learning experience for many of the revolutionaries in understanding firsthand the lives of the peasants.

As the guerrillas gained control, Batista sent more and more soldiers to the Sierra, but to no avail. Other guerrilla groups sprang up around the island. After a battle at Jigüe in May 1958, Batista's soldiers, demoralized, abandoned the Sierra. As the rebel force advanced westward and Che Guevara captured a troop train near Santa Clara in December, Batista's army collapsed. On January 1, 1959, Batista left for Santo Domingo, and a week later the revolutionaries entered Havana in triumph. Fidel was thirty-two years old, Che thirty, and they had a country to run.

Revolution

The first months of the Revolution were dizzying. Although the moderates Manuel Urrutia and José Miró Cardona were appointed president and prime minister, the "Granma group"—Fidel, his brother Raúl, Che Guevara, and a few others—were really at the helm. The brothels and casinos were closed, the long-awaited agrarian reform was initiated, racial equality was declared and all whites-only restrictions removed, rents were reduced and tenants given rights, and new ministries were formed to oversee the reforms—including the expropriation of the properties of Batista and his cronies and, increasingly, US-owned businesses. The sugar mills were nationalized by February 1960.

The Empire Strikes Back

These radical changes laid the foundation for the hostile standoff between the US and Cuba that has endured ever since. While the Cuban poor were jubilant, the US government was quick to react. As early as March 1959, it was secretly planning to overthrow Castro.

When the first shipment of Soviet crude oil in exchange for sugar arrived in Cuba in April 1960, US companies in Cuba, under pressure from their government, refused to refine it, so Fidel expropriated them. When the US retaliated by cutting its sugar import quota, the Soviet Union bought up the unsold sugar. In November, the US declared a trade embargo. Although the Soviet bloc helped plug the import gap, the embargo—still in force today, although eased slightly by President Barack Obama—created much hardship and drove the Cuban economy into a different dependence that would be exposed when the Soviet bloc itself disintegrated.

Economic Reform

Serious economic reform began in 1961. Che Guevara, in charge of the process, was an original thinker but not an economist or a manager. His ideas were radical and utopian, and many proved impossible to carry out. But Che also saw the need to diversify the island's economy away from the sugar monoculture. There was much debate about industrialization, but there were few trained economists left in Cuba. The new rulers had not realized the true cost of redistributing national wealth massively to the rural poor and ignoring the interests of educated urban professionals. Industrial expertise drained away, and the US embargo blocked access to industrial inputs and impeded the use of existing US-owned infrastructure. Soviet-made replacements of US equipment were less efficient and unfamiliar to the workforce. Given the circumstances, continued reliance on sugar and raw material production was the only realistic option.

The year 1961 saw the national literacy crusade, in which a million Cubans—men and women equally—particularly in remote rural areas, were taught to read and write by 100,000 young volunteer teachers. So bold and successful was this experiment that it caught the imagination of the world and became a defining symbol of the Cuban Revolution.

The Bay of Pigs

However, on April 17, 1961, just as the young teachers were heading for the remotest corners of Cuba with their exercise books and storm lanterns, about 1,400 anti-Castro Cuban exiles, sponsored and supported by the United States, invaded Cuba at the Bay of Pigs (Playa Girón) in the Zapata swamplands. The Cuban army defeated them within forty-eight hours, but from that moment on the country was defined as being in a constant state of military readiness against the United States. Fidel, in his funeral speech for the seven Cuban soldiers killed, for the first time clearly declared the Revolution and the Cuban state socialist.

The Missile Crisis

A year later, Cuba became the theater for one of the most alarming incidents of the Cold War, when Castro allowed the Soviet Union to deploy nuclear missiles on Cuban soil. A launch site was constructed and warheads had actually begun arriving when the US—warned of the missile deployment by a double agent in Soviet military intelligence—imposed a naval blockade on Cuba. The boats carrying warheads turned back and the missiles in Cuba were withdrawn, but for thirteen days the world

came breathtakingly close to nuclear war. The decision to stand down was made in a blizzard of letters between presidents Kennedy and Khrushchev, showing how easy it was for a small country to become a pawn in the deadly East–West power game.

In the Soviet Fold

Throughout the rest of the 1960s and the 1970s Cuba drew closer to the Soviet bloc and Cuban Communism was at its most orthodox. The Communist Party was restructured along stricter Marxist–Leninist lines as the Partido Comunista de Cuba (PCC) in 1965 and held its first Congress in 1975. In 1976, under the provisions of the new constitution introduced that year, the National Assembly of People's Power, the Cuban parliament, was established.

This was an unhappy period for intellectual life: civil rights were restricted, university departments were closed down, and writers and artists could not

publish even mild criticism of the socialist system. Though much art, literature, and particularly film was produced, the cultural adventurousness of the Revolution's earliest years was diluted, especially after 1968. In that year, Castro resoundingly criticized Alexander Dubcek's "Prague Spring" and outlawed small family businesses, the last remnants of private enterprise at home.

This was also the period of "exporting revolution" to other Third World countries. Cuba became involved in armed revolutionary struggles, for example in Nicaragua and Grenada, and in support of Soviet-backed regimes such as Ethiopia. From 1976 Cuban troops played a key role in Angola's civil war, defeating the South African forces at Cuito Cuanavale in 1988.

La Rectificación

In 1986 Castro launched a process called "rectification," declaring that the Revolution needed to return to socialist ethical values, moral incentives—and more efficient central planning. Meetings with the population were held over a year. Fidel stated on July 26, 1987, that rectification was "not idealism, but realism, better use of the economic management and planning system," and a correction of deviations "from the revolutionary spirit, from revolutionary work, revolutionary virtue, revolutionary effort, revolutionary responsibility." Typical of this approach was the abrupt closure, in May 1986, of the private farmers' and craft markets that had been allowed to open in the early 1980s, on the grounds that they were enticements to undue individual enrichment. Volunteer work brigades, used to good effect in the 1970s to confront housing shortages, were reintroduced, and the bureaucracy was slimmed down by thousands in 1988.

The Soviet Collapse and the Special Period

In 1989 the Berlin Wall fell and the world changed. Over the next few years Soviet aid and subsidies were withdrawn from Cuba and the countries of the disappearing "Eastern bloc" redirected their trade. As these props fell away, the Cuban government launched an austerity regime with the Orwellian title of "Special Period in Peacetime," aiming to keep the country afloat without caving in to the embargo or endangering Cuba's social achievements. Limited market-oriented reforms were made, mostly in agriculture and tourism. Cuba desperately sought new export products (sugar by-products, pharmaceuticals, and high-tech medical equipment) and new trading partners, and strove for self-sufficiency in food production and medical products. But fuel and other shortages soon made themselves felt: the transportation system collapsed, power outages became a daily irritant, and the lines at shops grew longer as the shelves got barer.

The Fourth Party Congress, in 1991, was unusually open and consultative and introduced some democratic reforms, such as secret ballots—though there was no talk of abandoning the one-party system. Greater powers were given to the elected National Assembly and several members of the revolutionary Old Guard were replaced with promising young Communists. Religious believers were admitted to the Party. Redefining isolation as independence, the leadership increasingly emphasized the homegrown nature of Cuban socialism. "No one gave us a revolution," Fidel told journalists in April 1990. "It wasn't imported from anywhere: we made it ourselves."

Exile the Cuban Way

Fighting for change in Cuba from somewhere else is a traditional Cuban form of protest: both José Martí and Fidel Castro employed it, and the anti-Castro Cuban exile community in the United States is among the most powerful pressure groups in the world (though it has not really managed to change anything in Cuba).

Apart from a steady trickle of "defectors," exodus on a grand scale has taken place twice since the early mass departures. In 1980, after a dialogue between Castro and Miami Cubans on the phased release of political prisoners and visits to Cuba by Cubans living abroad, thousands stormed the Peruvian embassy in Havana demanding asylum. Castro decided to allow people to leave from the port of Mariel. More than 125,000 did so before both countries replaced migration controls.

The US and Cuban exile groups accused Fidel of using the boatlift to remove some 2,800 criminals, homosexuals, mental patients, and other "undesirables" from Cuba's prisons and hospitals. The controversy inspired Oliver Stone to reimagine the 1932 gangster movie *Scarface* as a Mariel boatlift story, with Al Pacino in the role of Tony Montana, a small-time Cuban thug turned Miami gangster who dies in a hail of machine gun bullets.

In 1994, thousands more left on small boats and rafts in response to the hardships of the Special Period, prompting a sea change in US policy toward Cuban migration, allowing for controlled migration (20,000 visas a year) and the repatriation of Cuban "boat people" ineligible for political asylum.

Tourism Takes Over and Fidel Steps Down

By 1993 the economic crisis was deep. After exhaustive nationwide discussions, a series of reforms was introduced that effectively reshaped the Cuban economy: making the US dollar legal tender in Cuba, enabling (and taxing) self-employment, replacing the state farms with cooperatives and allowing the return of the farmers' markets, and extending the legislation governing joint ventures with foreign investors.

A new Ministry of Tourism was created in 1994 and by 1995 tourism revenues had replaced sugar as the country's principal source of foreign revenue. Huge foreign investment from Spain and Canada was channeled into an ambitious program of hotel building and tourist infrastructure that brought 10 million visitors to the island between 1990 and 2000, Canadians making up by far the largest group.

The government meanwhile, dropped the communist sloganeering and promoted an image of modernity and nationalism, justifying crackdowns on dissent by blaming destabilization efforts by the US, while continuing to court US administrations and demand an end to the US trade embargo.

Pope John Paul II, visiting the island in January 1998, implicitly praised Cuba for not taking the neoliberal capitalist road at the expense of its poor, while urging the regime to allow freedom of belief, "the basis of all other human rights." In response Fidel Castro publicly recognized the Church, which had been suppressed since the early 1960s, and allowed services, baptisms, and an increase in the clergy. However, Cuba continues to attract international criticism over its human rights record.

Speculation about the post-Castro future is Cuba-watchers' favorite game, but in fact Fidel gradually withdrew from hands-on government, temporarily stepping down from power in 2006 after undergoing serious colon surgery, and officially handing over power to his brother Raúl in February 2008.

THE POLITICAL SYSTEM

The One-Party State

Cuba is a one-party parliamentary republic, led by the Communist Party of Cuba (PCC). Although the definition of the state as Marxist–Leninist in the 1976 Constitution was removed in 1992, the PCC is the only legal political party. Party members and citizens involved in the mass organizations are consulted, but the Party makes the final decisions.

The president is both head of state and head of government. Fidel Castro was president from 1976—having been prime minister from 1959 until that date, when that office was abolished—until 2008. He was also president of the Councils of State and Ministers, first secretary of the PCC, commander-in-chief of the armed forces, and the National Assembly representative for Santiago de Cuba. When he stood down in 2008 for reasons of health, the National Assembly unanimously voted in his younger brother Raúl as president.

The thirty-one-member Council of State is elected by the National Assembly to exercise legislative power when the Assembly is not in session. Eight of its members form the Council of Ministers, the cabinet. The Assembly also elects the president.

Castro justified the one-party state by appealing to the overriding need for unity against US hostility. He believed Cuba would not be able to deal with the US threat if it were politically divided. In that sense the US stance hardened Fidel's determination not to allow pluralism. His successors may decide otherwise.

Parliament and Elections

The National Assembly of People's Power (Asamblea Nacional del Poder Popular) has 609 seats. Its members are elected directly from lists proposed and approved at constituency level. There is universal suffrage from the age of sixteen.

Elections for the 169 municipal assemblies are held every two and a half years, and general

(including presidential) elections every five years. By law, the PCC may not nominate candidates, and candidates do not have to be members of the Party, but in practice most of them are. Despite the introduction of the secret ballot in 1991, Fidel Castro was reelected president with the usual near-universal majority in subsequent elections.

After Fidel announced that due to illness he would no longer stand for office, in February 2008 his brother Raúl, as we've seen, was elected president by the National Assembly. Reelected in February 2013, he has said he will stand down in 2018.

The Mass Organizations

With the Communist Party in absolute control of politics, society, and the economy, the ability of social organizations to affect change is very limited. Cuba has a host of student organizations, women's organizations, trade unions, and farmers' associations, but they all answer to the state, which until the recent easing on restrictions on running private businesses was the only employer. Most controversial are the Committees for the Defense of the Revolution (CDRs), a national network of neighborhood-level committees created immediately before the Playa Girón incident to be the "eyes and ears of the Revolution."

Tropical Socialism?

Although fairly orthodox Marxist-Leninist, Soviet-style Communism held sway from the late 1960s to the early '80s, Cuban communism in practice had many specifically Latin American and idiosyncratic features. Fidel Castro can best be seen in the context of the paternalistic Latin American *caudillo*, a usually charismatic political-military leader who runs the country unchallenged, according to his whims and preferences. *Fidelismo* focused on Cuba's education and health care systems, which became the envy of some so-called First World countries, and drew heavily on the nationalist heritage of Martí and other revolutionary heroes like Che Guevara to create role models of socialist behavior.

The Cuban Revolution and post-revolution system of government basically came down to one man. That's why it was only when Fidel Castro stepped down in 2008 that Raúl Castro able to introduce reforms allowing a much wider system of private enterprise, private ownership of property, and to begin the negotiations with the US that led to the current thaw in Cuba–US relations.

The Human Rights Situation

Cuba's human rights record acutely illustrates the contradictions inherent in its political system. On the one hand Cuba attacks the US for its aggression abroad and treatment of racial minorities at home, and then justifies its own crackdown on dissent, censorship of publications that don't toe the party line, and imprisonment of critics. The situation has improved markedly since the early days after the Revolution, when supporters of Batista were lined up and shot, but freedom of religion and sexual orientation are relatively recent developments, and freedom of speech is severely limited.

Cuba has defended its rights record by highlighting the country's efforts to overcome long-standing poverty and discrimination in the face of US hostility, arguing that it could not allow destabilizing elements to derail the Revolution. Amnesty International has condemned the rights situation in the country but said that the US trade embargo, and especially US funding for "democracy building" in Cuba, has played into the government's hands, enabling it to lump all dissidents together as US sympathizers.

One element of the negotiations between Barack Obama and Raúl Castro before diplomatic relations were restored in 2015 was the US insistence that political prisoners had to be released, and fifty-three prisoners were freed. The debate on how much freedom is too much freedom continues. But with the easing of US trade and travel restrictions the argument that an embattled Cuba can brook no internal dissent rings increasingly hollow.

THE ECONOMY

Cuba has one of the few centrally planned economies still in existence and the state is still the number one employer. Sugar, the historical linchpin of the economy, is no longer the principal foreign exchange earner, having been replaced by tourism, remittances (money sent from Cubans abroad), and nickel.

Cuba is the world's sixth largest exporter of nickel and has 30 percent of the world's reserves. The Moa Bay mines in Holguín Province are the largest producer of nickel and is run by the Canadian firm Sherrit International, although Chinese and US mining firms have their eye on Cuba's extensive nickel and cobalt reserves.

Remittances have surged since restrictions on sending money from the US were eased by President Obama in 2011, with US $2.77bn sent to relatives in 2013 from the USA, Mexico, and Spain.

In the medical sector, Cuba exports biotechnology and pharmaceuticals, and is boosting its foreign exchange earnings by expanding into the lucrative market of health tourism, combining its reputation as a travel destination with its competitive pricing for procedures, and highly-trained medical professionals.

One of the main bilateral agreements keeping Cuba in fuel has been the oil-for-doctors deal signed with Venezuela's late president, Hugo Chavez, an unusual model of payment in which Cuba sends its doctors to work with the poor in Venezuela as a partial payment for oil shipments. The model has been replicated in other ALBA (Bolivarian Alliance for the Peoples of Our America) countries such as Ecuador, Bolivia, and Brazil.

Other exports that have seen an increase in recent years are tobacco, rum, seafood, citrus, and coffee.

A positive legacy of the Special Period has been the adoption of large-scale organic agriculture. The experiment was so successful that the whole country

has been converted to organic production, and it is now the only form of agriculture permitted by law.

After an estimated 35 percent contraction in 1990–93, and a dip in earnings in 2008 caused by the international economic crisis and a devastating hurricane season, the Cuban economy is now recovering, with growth of 2–3 percent a year expected to rise significantly in 2015–16 following the Cuba–US thaw.

From Full Employment to Self-Employment

Self-employment was made legal in 1993 to deal with the redundant labor force created by a drastic fall in sugar exports and cuts to state bureaucracy. It was initially restricted to family-run businesses and a small list of very specific activities. As the state has contracted the list of licensed activities has grown, and there now more than 500,000 licensed small entrepreneurs, or *cuenta propistas*. In the beginning, licenses were issued for running a *casa particular* (guesthouse) or *paladar* (small restaurant), fixing bicycles, and shining shoes, but the list has increased to include the buying and selling of property or cars.

Private enterprise has become increasingly important to the government as it provides tax revenue to help keep Cuba's vaunted health and education systems afloat. Introduced in 1996, income tax came as a shock to Cubans who had always relied on some small business activity or barter to supplement state wages or pensions. Cuba's income tax rate starts at 4 percent and rises to a ceiling of 50 percent, covering all annual income both in the country and abroad for Cubans, and income within Cuba for temporary residents. Corporate tax is lower, at 35 percent.

The other shock for Cubans has been the high price of food and clothing being sold in the private sector compared to the subsidized prices for rationed goods at state stores. The opening up of the economy to private enterprise has created a gulf between the majority of Cubans, who still rely on the state and can earn anything from US $15 to US $25 a month, and those in the private sector, especially those working with tourists, who can earn hundreds, even thousands of dollars a month.

The same is true with remittances, as many small businesses are being set up with seed money sent from relatives abroad. As the restrictions on sending money from the US are eased, the gulf between those who receive remittances and those who don't is having a profound affect on Cuban society. The most likely development of Cuba's economy in the future is toward a mixed economy with both socialist and capitalist features: a typically pragmatic and inventive Cuban solution.

LOOKING AHEAD: OBAMA'S BIG THAW AND THE FUTURE OF US–CUBA RELATIONS

It seems astonishing nowadays that the standoff between Fidel Castro's Cuba and the US that began in the 1960s has lasted so long. The US embargo has undoubtedly held back Cuba's economic and social development, and hurt US economic interests, but it has not brought down the Cuban regime, which has remained in place, an irritant to successive US governments. Now and then it seemed that "normalization" of relations might be possible, but the strong opposition to Fidel from the Cuban exile community in the key election state of Miami has exercised considerable influence on US government policy.

When President Barack Obama came to power in 2009 his administration was slow to move on Cuba. However, in December 2014, Obama and Raúl Castro announced the beginning of a process of normalizing relations between their countries.

After the US took Cuba off its list of State Sponsors of Terrorism in April 2015 and Cuba released fifty-three political prisoners, the two countries finally reestablished diplomatic ties. After more than fifty-four years of mutual hostility, in July 2015 Cuba reopened its embassy in Washington and the US reopened its embassy in Havana.

chapter **two**

VALUES & ATTITUDES

It has been called *Cubanía*, *Cubaneo*, or *Cubanidad*, but nobody has fully defined "Cuban-ness", or what it means to be Cuban. For the scholar Fernando Ortiz (1880–1969) *Cubanía is* the consciousness of being Cuban, and a will and desire to be Cuban that goes beyond mere ownership of a Cuban passport or birth certificate.

A patriotic nationalism that runs deeper than loyalty to socialism, it is rooted in the idiosyncracies of speech and the playful expressions that quickly identify a speaker as Cuban, the deep culture of music and dance that pervade every aspect of life, the diet of pork, beans, and plantains that gourmet critics may sneer at but which Cubans drool over, the witty banter known as "*choteo*" that brings a smile even in the face of hardship, and the sensual "swing" that Cuban hips—both male and female—have as they walk down the street.

One reason why independence hero Jose Martí strikes so strong a chord with Cubans everywhere is not just because he died fighting for the freedom of his country, but also because he expressed a deep and moving nostalgia for all things Cuban in the poems he wrote as an exile in the US.

The fierce pride that Cubans feel for their island home was undoubtedly forged in conflict, during the long struggle for independence, but Cuban identity is tied to much more than a longing for freedom. *Cubanía* is also about the undimmed Cuban spirit of defiance, the resilience and patience that have got the Cuban people through tough times, and the hope that the future will be better.

RESILIENCE AND RESOURCEFULNESS

Cubans have been immensely inventive and resilient throughout their history. They are experts at making do and mending—a quality that got them through the harsh austerities of the Special Period. A classic example of this is the way vintage US cars and Chinese bicycles are kept running despite a lack of spares.

The same ingenuity and inventiveness can be seen in the experiments in ecological conservation, recycling, and especially organic agriculture, that were launched in the Special Period from necessity and which now are hailed as models of sustainability that are being emulated abroad.

Cubans also possess the spirit of enterprise. Even during the 1980s little businesses would spring up at the slightest opportunity, even if they were closed down a couple of weeks later. The legalization of self-employment in 1993 caused an immediate rush of small business registrations; some of these micro-businesses almost certainly already existed clandestinely.

Since the thaw with the US, even more avenues are opening to Cuban entrepreneurs. The results can be seen in the tiny *paladres* being converted into organic, pop-up-style restaurants that would be the envy of New York or London, or *casas particulares* converted into upmarket boutique hotels.

THE SPIRIT OF THE REVOLUTION

Patriotism

"*¡Cuba, qué linda es Cuba!*—"Cuba, how beautiful Cuba is!"—says Cuba's unofficial national anthem, and the verse sums up the Cubans' deeply felt patriotism. Cubans are devoted to their country, and most can't see why anyone would want to live anywhere else—though of course many of them do, in American "Little Havanas" where they do their best to recreate the look, the taste, and the sounds of Cuba itself.

There is still great pride in the achievements of the Revolution. Even critics do not want to lose its social and cultural advances. Younger people cannot imagine life without free education and health care, so they complain about other things, like the absence of consumer goods or lack of access to high-speed Internet. An ability to condemn individuals but not institutions, is common: people tend to blame "the bureaucracy" rather than the government.

Many Cubans in all walks of life are committed to the socialist regime and the kind of society it has produced. They feel that what they lack in terms of material possessions is made up for by their cultural wealth, and endure considerable hardship at home rather than seek prosperity abroad, even taking a puritanical view of livelihoods on the margins of legality. One thing that surprises visitors to the island is that there are many voices in Cuba, and that everyone sticks passionately to their point of view.

Heroes and Symbols

Martí is a powerful symbol of the *patria* for Cubans, and both the government and the exile community have made use of this: the exiles by setting up Radio Martí to beam anti-Castro propaganda at Cuba, and the government by tactically downplaying socialism and invoking Martí to appeal to nationalist sentiments. Fidel Castro is still idolized by some, especially the aging but still numerous generation of those he liberated.

The hero whose name is constantly invoked, not just in official rhetoric but in everyday discourse and on billboards throughout the country, is the young Argentine doctor and revolutionary Ernesto "Che" Guevara. Executed in Bolivia in 1967 while, unsuccessfully, trying to launch a Cuban-style revolution there, his beret-clad and bearded face is immortalized on a million T-shirts.

Community and Cooperation

The Cubans' sense of community, already strong before the Revolution, has been nurtured since 1959, not only by the creation of neighborhood committees and mass organizations, but by the sharing of dramatic experiences of both prosperity and adversity. In particular, the sudden sharp downturn in living standards after 1989, which affected everybody, united citizens rather than producing the predicted collapse of society. Many foreigners are impressed by this community spirit and by the ease with which Cubans value collective interests often over their own individual interests. The neighborhood is important, and people cooperate naturally, helping and looking out for each other.

Cubans treat each other—and visitors—with courtesy but not deference. The revolutionary form of address, *Compañero* (Comrade), is still widely used. Cubans may seek money and material comfort, but on the whole they do not seek social status, and are unpretentious. The gap between the highest and lowest earners is still relatively small, though it is widening much further with the loss of state jobs and the opening of private enterprise.

DISSENT

Paradoxically for such a nation of patriots, Cubans are also quick to vote with their feet. The tendency of serious anti-Castroists to leave the country rather than stay at home and organize an internal opposition may also help to explain the regime's longevity. Internal opposition is vocal but is not very organized and is therefore weak and ineffectual. Though you may hear plenty of complaints from people you meet in Cuba, it is actually very difficult to get hard, objective evidence of the "opposition movement," not only because it naturally excites extreme passions in Cubans on either side but because the Cuban penchant for both secrecy and exaggeration often gets in the way of the truth.

Bitching About Bureaucracy

The kind of dissent that gets people arrested is not the same thing, however, as grumbling about the government and particularly bureaucracy, which has been a national sport ever since the 1960s. Cubans tend to blame obtuse, rule-bound bureaucrats for every problem that can't be attributed to the US embargo. At the same time they can be infuriatingly bureaucratic themselves, once installed behind a desk, as anyone who has hung around Havana airport waiting for a non-standard visa to be stamped can attest.

Fidel himself made complaining about the bureaucracy legitimate when he declared in a speech to the National Assembly in 1993 that the civil service "must be streamlined." The absurdities of bureaucracy have been the subject of comic critique in Cuban films such as *Death of a Bureaucrat* (1966) and *Guantanamera* (1995). In fact, Cubans are always kicking in small ways against their nanny state, finding ways around rules or simply ignoring them.

The legions of people who offer services to tourists that are strictly speaking illegal is a very visible example; but a broad streak of anarchism goes back at least to the early workers' movement and the influence of anarcho-syndicalist Spanish immigrants in the first years of the twentieth century, and has helped to temper the Cuban brand of socialism.

ATTITUDES TOWARD RACE

Cuba is a true meltingpot of races that includes traces of the original Taínos and the Spanish conquistadors who took their island by force, the more than 1 million slaves brought from Africa, exiled French plantation owners from Haiti, Chinese indentured laborers, and Soviet bloc visitors who came for the sun in the 1970s and '80s and stayed. Intermarriage has been common for centuries, and up to 70 percent of the population is estimated to be of mixed race. Cuban culture owes a tremendous amount to this kaleidoscopic heritage.

Declaring racial equality was one of the first acts of the Revolution and legislation to abolish "whites only" discrimination was quickly passed. Older black Cubans who lived through segregation still praise Fidel Castro for abolishing it. But, though racial discrimination no longer exists officially, in practice it is all too alive.

The Revolution gave black Cubans health care, education, and decent employment, but—despite the departure of many rich whites—light-skinned Cubans continued to run the show. Indeed nearly all the revolutionary leaders were white. Even now few black Cubans have top jobs, though there are some rising political stars and many black professionals such as doctors and university professors.

In the well-paid tourist sector—where a single tip to a bellboy in foreign currency can exceed the monthly wage of a doctor—lighter-skinned Cubans are more likely to find employment. Also, as it was mainly white, middle-class Cubans who chose to leave Cuba after the Revolution and it is their remittances to family members on the island that are providing the cash injection to get new businesses started, a new class divide is forming in the country between those with access to foreign currency and those stuck in the state sector.

For years, the government argument that racism had been eliminated meant it was considered counter-revolutionary to bring up the issue. Anti-racist legislation meant that while there could be no whites-only clubs or meeting places, there could be no blacks-only ones either, making it hard for black people to discuss racism together.

Since the late 1990s, however, Cuban academics and government officials have begun to look again at the issue of race. Fidel Castro's presence at the UN World Conference on Racism held in Durban in 2001 gave the green light for wider discussion of the topic. Young black people are now using rap music to denounce racism and there is an emerging awareness of race issues on the island.

ATTITUDES TOWARD RELIGION

The Cuban state "recognizes, respects and guarantees religious freedom," according to the Constitution, but when the Catholic Church spoke out against Fidel Castro's regime, it retaliated by closing Church schools, many churches, and limiting the numbers of priests. Protestant churches and synagogues came under the same prohibitions and Jehovah's Witnesses were banned outright in 1975.

Catholicism has quietly survived, but Cuba was never as fervently Catholic as some other countries in Latin America, due in part to the enduring strength of Afro-Cuban religions. Since the Church was officially re-recognized in 1998, the number of Cubans interested in Christian religious practice and values has been growing. People who had abandoned or hidden their Catholicism are returning to the Church.

Neither the crackdown on Catholicism nor economic hardship, however, has dimmed the national devotion to the Virgin of El Cobre, the Patroness of Cuba, who holds a special place in the heart of the nation, being at once an expression of the Catholic worship of the Virgin Mary, a manifestation of Ochun, the *orisha* of love and dancing, and a national icon.

Judaism was severely restricted for many years—most of Cuba's 15,000 Jews fled when Castro took power—but the community is now reemerging and there are synagogues in Havana and Camagüey.

The Muslim community is about 4,000 strong, mostly of Lebanese descent, and includes Cuban converts. There is no mosque as yet in Cuba, although Muslims in Havana have a prayer room at the Casa Arabe, a museum of Arabic culture. Saudi Arabia has pledged the cash to build a mosque in Havana but it awaits a green light from the state.

Afro-Cuban Religion

The religion of the Yoruba people came to Cuba in the ships bringing African slaves and evolved over the centuries into the Afro-Cuban religion known as Santería or Regla de Ocha. For a long time it was a clandestine activity, with ceremonies and rituals held in private houses in the poorer neighborhoods of Havana or deep in the countryside. Nowadays it is found everywhere and is practiced by Cubans of every color, age, political persuasion, and walk of life.

Popular Cuban songs often include references to the *orishas* (see pages 65–7), and one of the most popular international Cuban hip hop acts was actually called Orishas. Cuban films regularly include scenes of Santería rituals and Abakuá dances feature in the repertoire of the national folk dance company.

In the last ten years shelves of books have been published on Afro-Cuban lore and religion, further raising its profile, and curious tourists, for a fee, can easily arrange a visit to a Santería ceremony—with chanting, dancing, and drums.

Away from the spectacle of Santería as theater there is a growing movement to rescue Afro-Cuban religion from folklore, disentangle it from Christian syncretisms, and recover its original values and traditional practices.

MEN AND WOMEN

An image of Cuba prevalent among tourists, particularly men, is that it is a permissive place, where sex is always on the agenda and women are bold and willing. It is true that Cubans talk volubly and frankly about sex, as about most things; but these attitudes are highly colored by a pervasive *machismo*.

At the same time, sexual life is conditioned by the Revolution's genuine desire to promote equality between men and women. Thus the divorce rate is high, consensual unions are common, and the availability of abortion lightens the pressure on people to avoid pre- or extramarital sex.

Cuban women are more independent than in many other developing countries: they have jobs and incomes and the state provides child care, so they are not economically chained to unsatisfactory relationships. Yet family life is very important to Cubans. The culture idealizes motherhood and children, and most young women want to find a husband and have a family. Women who become *jineteras* (prostitutes) usually do so for harsh economic reasons.

Cuban *machismo* has been called the worst in Latin America. Its historical roots lie in the days of slavery, when women were owned as property and slave owners had sexual rights over them. A masculine culture of multiple partners and domestic violence persists, despite legislation and policies for equality such as the Family Code of 1975 and more recent measures to tackle domestic violence.

LGBT CUBANS COME OUT OF THE COLD WAR CLOSET

As a sign of how far LGBT rights have advanced in Cuba in the last few years, over 1,000 lesbian, gay, bisexual, and transgender Cubans marched through Havana in May 2015 in the 8th Annual March against Homophobia and Transphobia. The marchers were calling for the legalization of same-sex marriage, but although the march was a protest, it was also a celebration of LGBT pride. Perhaps the most surprising aspect of the march is that it was organized by President Raúl Castro's daughter, Mariela Castro, who called for an end to all discrimination based on sex, race, or religion.

Mariela is a heterosexual mother of three who has been championing LGBT rights since she was made head of the Cuban National Center for Sex Education (CENESEX) in 2000. CENESEX gives sex education classes, HIV prevention advice, and free condoms, and works with families and community groups to increase LGBT acceptance. Mariela successfully lobbied for transgender people to receive free sex reassignment surgery in the Cuban health system, which became law in 2008. Workplace discrimination based on sexual orientation was banned in 2013.

It's quite a change from the early years of the Revolution when homosexuals were regularly imprisoned, an experience brought vividly to life by the poet Reinaldo Arenas in his autobiography *Antes Que Anochezca* (Before Night Falls). Perhaps inspired by Mariela Castro's efforts on behalf of the LGBT community, Fidel Castro admitted in 2010 that sending homosexuals to labor camps had been "a great injustice" and stated that homosexuality is a "natural aspect and tendency of human beings."

You will still hear hurtful insults like *maricón* (gay) bandied about, as elsewhere in Latin America, but the greater acceptance of gay culture in Cuban society, combined with the island's beautiful beaches, sensual music, and tropical weather, has seen a boom in recent years in tourism packages aimed at the LGBT community, and there is a vibrant if discreet gay scene in both Havana and Santiago de Cuba.

HOT HABANEROS COOL ON COUNTRYSIDE

The inhabitants of Havana, or Habaneros, are proud that they live in the biggest, busiest and most developed city on the island and can be dismissive of other parts of Cuba, which they often refer to as *el campo* (the countryside).

With access to nearby beaches, the Malecón promenade and sea wall, and hip Vedado district for hanging out, free art shows, ballet, theater, and music concerts nearly every night of the week, it's easy to see where this cosmopolitan pride originates.

ATTITUDES TOWARD FOREIGNERS

Cubans are unfailingly welcoming to foreign visitors—surprisingly, perhaps, given the way tourism has once again limited their access to places where the well-off play—and treat them with intense curiosity and interest.

For many years Cubans were well acquainted with nations and people about whom the Western world knew little—as Russians, Bulgarians, Czechs, Yugoslavs, East Germans. But, although the Soviet Union was Cuba's economic savior for three decades, the Cubans were never particularly fond of Eastern Europeans—particularly Russians—or their culture, and they were often treated privately as figures of fun. At the same time, they felt cut off from Western Europe and tended to quiz visitors mercilessly about it. They still do.

Much greater cultural affinity is expressed with both Latin America and the USA. Attitudes toward Latin Americans vary according to country and tend to be colored by a country's politics; Mexico in particular is seen as a bastion of solidarity. But there is a general view among Cubans that in terms of education, health, and social welfare they are much better off than people in other countries, and have a slight sense of superiority for that reason.

Culturally, Cuba's recognition of the links with other Caribbean countries is strong. To many black and mixed-race Cubans, Africa represents an ancestral homeland, and the growth of Afro–Cuban studies reflects this heritage.

Not surprisingly, Cuban views of the USA are complex. While political opposition is one of the things that unite Cuban citizens, opinions of the US people are more nuanced and sensitive.

Cubans responded to Hurricane Katrina in 2005 by expressing solidarity with the poor, and especially the black, population of the affected areas. Practically everyone in Cuba has relatives or friends living in the States, and Cuban culture is very American, a legacy of the years of American colonization, which is when much of the current urban infrastructure was built.

The passion for baseball (*beisbol*) and the persistence of American names for things, such as "Chevy" for a taxi, "blumers" for panties, "pulover" for sweater, and "cake" for, well, cake, hint at this cultural affinity. Cubans are fascinated by American consumer goods, music, and fashion trends, and popular US TV series from *The Big Bang Theory* to *Breaking Bad* are passed from person to person through hard-drives, in an informal distribution system known as *El Paquete*.

As the ties grow closer, the US influence on Cuban culture will only grow, although don't expect visible signs of US culture like Starbucks cafés or the golden arches of McDonald's any time soon.

chapter **three**

CUSTOMS & TRADITIONS

Africans, Europeans, and people of mixed descent have lived side by side, though not on equal terms, in Cuba for nearly five centuries. Cuban culture is a complex blend of traits brought here from Spain, from Catholic practice and tradition, and from Africa. In 1975 Fidel Castro declared the country to be "Afro-Latin," and it is increasingly recognized that Afro-Cuban culture and religion are central to Cuba's identity, to its music and dance.

Grafted on to this heritage is the official culture of the Revolution, which over the last fifty years has established a set of cultural practices and landmarks that has drawn on key events from the nineteenth-century independence wars and the Revolution to form a permanent background to people's lives.

CATHOLIC TRADITIONS

Cuba inherited the Catholic calendar from Spain, full of dramatic characters and colorful ceremonies, penances, prayers, sacrifices, and days of feasting and fasting. Manifestations of the Virgin Mary and the saints were particularly popular. Some traditions persisted after the Revolution despite the suppression of the Church, especially that of the Virgin of Charity of El Cobre, Cuba's patron Saint.

Now that the Church can operate openly again many religious traditions are re-emerging. Christmas Day was restored as a public holiday after a direct request by Pope John Paul II during his 1998 visit to the island, and Good Friday was made a public holiday after Pope Benedict XVI's visit.

Easter, Epiphany, and other key religious feasts and saints' days in the Christian year, are celebrated only in churches. Other traditions being revived

LA VIRGEN DE LA CARIDAD DEL COBRE

The story goes that some time between 1604 and 1612 two Indian brothers and a black slave boy were heading by boat to Nipe Bay to collect salt when a violent storm rocked their boat, and they prayed to the Virgin Mary for help. Miraculously the storm abated and they found a board bearing a small statue of the Virgin of Charity floating on the waves.

The statue was taken to the mine at El Cobre, near Santiago de Cuba, where a shrine was built for it and, in 1926, a large basilica.

In 1916, at the request of veterans of the Cuban Wars of Independence, the Virgin of Charity of El Cobre was declared Cuba's official patron saint by Pope Benedict XV. In true Cuban style she even has a nickname, and is affectionately known as "La Cachita."

Devotion to the Virgen del Cobre has never dimmed, even during the high revolutionary period, and she has long been linked with Cuba's struggles for freedom. In Miami, the Cuban

include the old Spanish Maytime Pilgrimage of the Cross (Romerías de la Cruz de Mayo), preserved in Holguín, where devotees climb 450 steps leading up to a cross overlooking the city. Many saints' days, particularly those of local patron saints, are marked with masses and street celebrations. Havana celebrates the feast of its patron saint, St. Christopher, with a solemn mass in the cathedral, and on Good Friday in Trinidad there is a traditional parade through the colonial streets of the city marking the Stations of the Cross.

community have a replica of the statue, in a shrine known as La Ermita de la Caridad.

In Santería she is equated with Oshún, the goddess of love, wealth, and fresh water, one of the most popular *orishas*, or gods. It is no coincidence that the tiny statue is always dressed in yellow or gold, the colors of Oshún.

On the feast day of the Virgin on September 8 pilgrims dress in yellow and flock to El Cobre from all over the island as the statue of the Virgin is carried in procession through the streets.

When the American novelist Ernest Hemingway wanted to dedicate his 1954 Nobel Prize for Literature to the Cuban people—because he had written *For Whom the Bell Tolls* and *The Old Man and the Sea* while in Cuba—he did so by placing his Nobel gold medal at her shrine. In 1986 the medal was stolen, sparking outrage. After Raúl Castro made a nationwide appeal it was promptly returned, something devotees of La Cachita see as another of the Virgin's miracles.

AFRO-CUBAN TRADITIONS

The African religions that put down roots in Cuba—chiefly that of the Yoruba slaves and their descendants—were shaped by the need for secrecy, to avoid persecution by the Catholic authorities for heresy or idolatory.

A syncretic religion called La Regla de Ochá, or La Regla de Lucumí, developed where African deities called *orishas* were associated with Catholic saints. It is known as Santería (lit. worship of saints) but in reality, devotees worship their own pantheon, which

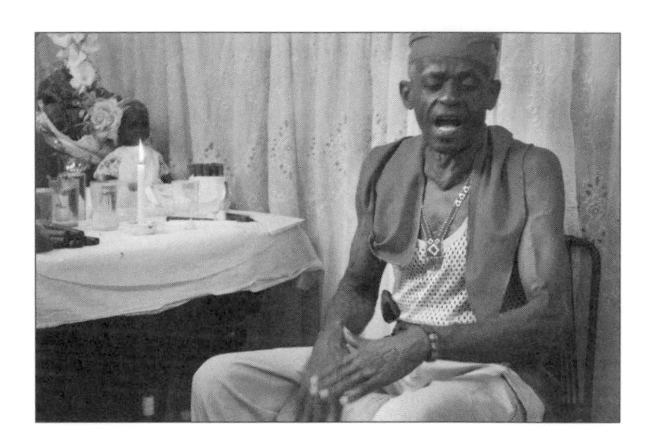

contains as many as four hundred regional or tribal *orishas*.

Elegguá, the first god to be invoked during ceremonies, was associated with the Holy Child of Atocha; Obatalá, the maker of human beings, is associated with the Immaculate Conception or the Virgin of Mercy; Yemayá, the goddess of the sea, with the Virgin of Regla, the patron saint of the port of Havana; Changó, the god of lightning bolts, thunder, and war but also of music and dance, with Saint Barbara.

The supreme deity in the Yoruba religion has three aspects, Olodumare, Olofi, and Olorún, and is associated with the Catholic Holy Trinity.

The priests, called *babalawos*, undergo rigorous initiation and training. Rituals are performed in the home—a legacy of the history of concealment—where decorated altars are set up. Music and dance are central to Santería rituals, with songs for each *orisha*, and dances reflecting their qualities. The percussive rhythms of Santería ceremonies have played an integral part in the development of Cuban music, most notably in *rumba* and *son*. During a ceremony a celebrant may be possessed by the god invoked. The sacrifice of small animals is a feature of the ceremonies.

The practice of Santería is so ingrained in Cuban life that you hear many expressions that come directly from the religion in popular music and on the street, like *bilongo* (a spell), and *aché*, which refers to the essential life force or power of the *orishas*, but which is used as a way to say "Bless you!" in everyday speech.

Other Afro-Cuban cults are the Palo Monte (the Rule of Mayombé), introduced to Cuba by Congolese and Angolan slaves and based on the cult of the dead; and Abakuá, not strictly speaking a religion but a secret society open only to men, which became dominated by whites and earned a sinister reputation for violence under Batista. Today, Abakuá is closer to a kind of Afro-Cuban freemasonry. The masked and hooded *diablito* (little devil), a figure from Abakuá ceremonies, has become part of Cuban folklore.

CELEBRATING HISTORY

Cuba shares with other socialist societies an enthusiasm for political and historical anniversaries and for naming days and years. Every year since 1959 has been given a name, for example, "Year of the Agrarian Reform" (1960), "Year of the Heroic Guerrilla" (1968, the year after Che's death), "Year of Institutionalization" (1977), "Year of the 30th Anniversary of the Granma Landing" (1986). The difficulty of maintaining this pattern is illustrated by 2005's title, "Year of the Bolivarian Alternative for the Americas."

Similarly, the calendar bristles with revolutionary feast days marked with speeches and rallies. They commemorate events such as the birthday of José Martí (January 28), the 1895 War of Independence (February 24), the Bay of Pigs incident (April 19), the death of Che Guevara (October 6), of Camilo Cienfuegos (October 28), and the Martyrs of the Revolution (June 30), and key battles in the independence wars and the revolutionary struggle. There are days in honor of women (International Women's Day, March 8), children (April 4), teachers (December 22), and others.

CULTURAL EVENTS

As part of its promotion of culture and of the nation, the government sponsors dozens of festivals devoted to film, music, dance, books, and Afro-Cuban culture. Some are annual, some biennial; some are international in scope, such as the international book or film festivals (see opposite), some extremely local, such as the festival of the cockerel in the town of Morón or the grapefruit harvest festival at Nueva Gerona on the Isle of Youth. Specialist festivals, such as the festival of steam, based in old sugar mills and factories, draw international enthusiasts. Cuba also hosts national and international conferences throughout the year, often on medical or scientific subjects.

SOME CULTURAL FESTIVALS

February–March: Havana International Book Fair.

April: PERCUBA—international percussion and drum festival, Havana.

May: Festival de Baile—dance, Santiago de Cuba.
May Festival—traditional music and dance, Holguín.

June: Festival Boleros de Oro—concerts by Cuban and international performers of *bolero* songs, Havana, Santiago, and Morón.

June, biennially: Jornada Cucalambeana, Encuentro Iberoamericano de la Décima—Cuban country music and poetry, Las Tunas.

August: Cubadanza—contemporary dance, Havana.
Festival de Rap Cubana, Havana Hip Hop–Alamar.

August, biennially: Festival Internacional de Música Popular "Benny Moré"—honoring this popular musician, Cienfuegos, Lajas, and Havana.

September, biennially: Matamoros Son—festival of *son* music.

October: Havana International Ballet Festival—Ballet Nacional de Cuba hosts international companies at this biennial festival.

November: Festival de Raíces Africanas Wemilere—government-sponsored Afro-Cuban festival, Guanabacoa.

December: International Festival of New Latin American Cinema, Havana.
Havana International Jazz Festival, Havana.
Fiesta a la Guantanamera—Afro-Cuban and French-Haitian music, culture, and folklore, Guantánamo.

PUBLIC HOLIDAYS

Until Christmas Day was reinstated as an official public holiday in 1998, all Cuba's public holidays commemorated political and historical events, chiefly with speeches, rallies, and gatherings in towns and cities. There are only a few official public holidays when offices and shops close (although most restaurants and tourist facilities function as normal). New Year's Day is celebrated countrywide, because it coincides with the anniversary of the day of liberation and the end of the Batista dictatorship. International Labor Day brings out the most participants, and rallies and marches are held everywhere. In Havana thousands of banner-waving students and mass organization members march past the president in front of the Martí monument in Havana's Plaza de la Revolución, but the crowds that once topped a million have dwindled in recent years. Similar events on a smaller scale mark July 26, the anniversary of the assault on the Moncada barracks, and October 10, the anniversary of the start of the Ten Years' War, the first major struggle for Cuban independence.

Public transportation is more unreliable than ever on public holidays, but on May 1 cavalcades of buses shuttle people to the mass rallies in every city and town.

CARNIVALS

Cuban Carnaval (Carnival), like so much of Cuban popular culture, has its roots in the slave era and the rare moments when slaves were allowed to participate in street *fiestas*. In the nineteenth century the end of the sugar harvest was celebrated with processions in

PUBLIC HOLIDAYS
January 1: Triumph of the Revolution/ Liberation Day
January 2: Victory of Armed Forces Day
January 28: Birthday of José Martí
Variable: Good Friday
May 1: Labor Day
July 25: National Revolutionary Festival
July 26: National Revolutionary Festival
July 27: National Revolutionary Festival
October 10: Independence Day
December 25: Christmas
December 31: Year End Celebration

which dancing troupes known as *comparsas* would compete. This developed into the present Carnaval at the turn of the twentieth century, with competing teams dancing through the streets in masks and colorful costumes and carrying banners and paper lanterns.

Before 1959 private companies sponsored *comparsas* from different neighborhoods, but after that, instead of consumer goods, they found themselves advertising revolutionary policies.

During the Special Period most annual celebrations were suspended, but Carnaval is now regaining its former glory. Carnaval bands use several kinds of drums, including the *tumba francesa*, brought from Haiti by the slaves of exiled French planters, and the *corneta china*, the Chinese cornet or trumpet, a late-nineteenth-century introduction. Looming over the parades are large gaudy floats carrying giant papier-mâché animals or human caricatures.

Havana has two carnivals a year, one in February and the main one in July and August, when top bands play nightly to dense crowds along the Malecón, the city's broad seafront promenade, and elsewhere around the city. The highlight, on the final weekend, is a spectacular parade of floats that winds its way from Old Havana down the Malecón.

Santiago de Cuba hosts Cuba's most lavish carnival in June, with splendidly costumed parades and floats, all-night music, and parties. The entire city is illuminated and all doors are decorated.

Camagüey has a smaller but still exciting and colorful version, also in June, and there are other carnivals at Pinar del Río (July), Ciego de Ávila (March, rather tourist oriented), and Varadero (late January to early February, unalloyed tourism).

CHRISTMAS CARNIVAL

A highly popular carnival-like event lasting for much of Advent is the Parrandas de Remedios, held in Remedios and neighboring villages from December 16 to 26. Originating in 1829, when the parish priest of Remedios got the village children to bang on sheets of tin to wake up the inhabitants for Advent masses, the festival begins with a children's parade and culminates in a contest between two quarters of the town, San Salvador and Carmen, to make the most noise. The Christmas Eve festivities culminate with a massive firework display, but never before the wee hours.

SECULAR WEDDING PALACES

The economic hardships of the 1990s have not dampened Cubans' enthusiasm for weddings—and ends can always be made to meet for the celebration. The revolutionary government established an institution for secular weddings, the Palacio de los Matrimonios, opening the first "palace" in a former gambling hall in Havana in 1966. The wedding ceremony at a *palacio* takes only fifteen minutes, and

successive wedding groups cross each other on the *palacio*'s broad stairs.

The simplest celebrations involve a rented wedding dress, homemade cake, and a pooling of the modest allocations of food, beer, and rum available on ration books. As tourism and remittances have grown, better off families have begun to splurge on more luxurious celebrations, with expensive dresses, caterers, and cars.

SWEET FIFTEEN

For girls in all Latin American countries, the fifteenth birthday (*los quince*) is a special event, signifying the young girl's entry into womanhood. Cuba is no exception. Typically, the birthday girl (*la quinceañera*) is fêted with a banquet, complete with big cake, at which she dances formally with her father and male relatives, and then with her boyfriend or a male friend. Fifteenth-birthday celebrations—often very ostentatious ones—were popular in Cuba until the Revolution, but then became lower-key. However, families still dig deep into their pockets to give their daughters a special event. Photographs and videos of the *quinceañera* in a variety of costumes are usually taken.

In recent years expensive *quinces* have made a comeback, often with financial help from well-off relatives abroad, and the celebratory mass is being held again. Weddings, baptisms, and funerals are also increasingly being celebrated in church since 1998.

chapter **four**

MAKING FRIENDS

Meeting the intensely social, chatty, and flirty Cubans couldn't be easier. Conversations are started over a trifle, and just as quickly teeth are flashed, intimacies swapped, personal space invaded, and hugs or kisses exchanged. It's a far cry from the stilted conversations, awkward silences, and frosty handshakes you might encounter in Canada or northern Europe, for example.

Foreign visitors from Canada, the US, and the UK, should be aware that this is just the norm, a natural product of a curious, gregarious people who live in large families, spend a lot of time outside interacting with neighbors, and who cultivate large networks of acquaintances, because that's what you need to get anything done in Cuba.

People here don't have the luxury of shutting themselves up in houses equipped with all the mod cons, dealing only with close nuclear family, and work colleagues, and if they did they'd probably die of boredom.

Visitors should be aware that not all approaches are genuine, of course, just as in any popular tourist destination there are *jineteros* (street hustlers) and *jineteras* (good-time girls) in places like Havana, Varadero, Santiago de Cuba, and Trinidad, whose sole aim is liberate what they see as "rich" foreigners from some of their excess cash. So it's wise to exercise some initial caution in your relationships with Cubans, but also to enjoy the pleasure of meeting people who are so immediate in their friendships.

MEETING PEOPLE

The Cuban way of life is very accessible to foreigners, and even more so if you prepare yourself with some basic Spanish before you arrive. Much of life is lived on the street or in the open doorway, and people are genuinely interested in each other. Even in the crowded center of Havana, it is impossible to feel anonymous, as you might do in most large Western cities: people will make eye contact as they pass, and someone will soon begin talking to you. If you ask for directions to a place, you are very likely to be taken there, especially if your Spanish isn't good. "Stranger danger" doesn't seem to be a Cuban concept. This kindness is all the more remarkable since the preferential treatment of foreigners has recreated some of the inequalities the Revolution abolished.

However, if you don't like being asked personal questions, don't go to Cuba. Everyone will ask where you come from and will want to know all about you. It's well-intentioned and understandable, particularly from people who have not themselves traveled. The wonderful spirit of neighborhood and community and the lack of privacy are two sides of the same coin.

Hospitality

Cubans are pathologically hospitable, and are quite likely to invite you home the first time they meet you, insisting that you share their meal or stay the night. If you want to refuse, it may be hard to know how to do so gracefully! If you do accept such an invitation, however, you should try to find a way to contribute something to the meal, or bring a small gift, and be prepared to reciprocate. If you eat out together, you should bear in mind that the relationship between you and your Cuban friends will be economically unequal, and be prepared to pay for the meal and drinks.

Right on Time

Should you arrive on time at someone's home? It's actually perfectly polite to be a little late—but not too late. Cubans' unpunctuality is legendary, but in fact they tend to be punctual when it matters, and not when it doesn't. Fluid timekeeping in social life is very understandable, especially considering that one can be penalized for arriving even ten minutes late at work, however bad the transportation.

One way to clarify how punctual you should be is the expression: "*Hora Britanico*?" (British time?). The question will raise a smile, and if answered in the positive is a clear indication that you should be no more than fifteen to twenty minutes late. Conversely if you are waiting for a Cuban friend to go for a drink, for dancing, or on a date, you should give them at least thirty minutes to an hour past the agreed time before giving up.

WHAT TO WEAR

A combination of warm climate and scarce resources means that dress in Cuba is usually very informal by European or North American standards, and can seem minimal to visitors from colder climes.

Cuban women are very careful about their appearance at the office and in the evening, and tend to dress up more than men. Trousers are as acceptable for women as skirts and dresses. At the beach and in informal settings, crop tops and short-shorts are the norm.

TOPLESS TABOO, CLOTHING-OPTIONAL CAYOS

Cuban women do not go topless as a rule and it is best to refrain from topless bathing on public Cuban beaches to show respect. The exceptions are the resort islands of Cayo Coco and Cayo Santa Maria in the Jardines del Rey archipelago, where for several years naturists have been able to enjoy clothing-optional bathing along specific stretches of beach.

Men sometimes wear tropical-weight suits or jackets at business meetings or official events, but the best investment you can make is to buy a *guayabera*—a classic Cuban shirt. Said to have originated in central Cuba, where workers picking guavas (*guayabas*) needed pockets to hold the fruit, the *guayabera* has short or long sleeves, two or four patch pockets, decorative vertical bands on the front, and mother-of pearl buttons. It's designed to be worn loose, and the long sleeve version in white or light blue is acceptable to wear on even the most formal of occasions.

On the whole, the watchword for the visitor is well-groomed informality. It is never tactful to dress with ostentatious expense.

CONVERSATION STARTERS AND STOPPERS

Cubans are talkative, so initiating conversation is no problem at all. Cubans use *choteo* (lighthearted humor) to keep things from getting too heavy. If you initiate a conversation, keep it light and stick to neutral topics or the kind of things Cubans can feel unequivocally proud of, such as the music, film, sporting achievements, or natural beauty of the country.

It might feel like a grilling but Cubans are naturally curious and will get straight to the point when it comes to asking you about where you are from, whether you are single or married, how many kids you have, why you have come to Cuba, and where you intend to visit.

You are also almost certain to be asked if you like Cuba. This is not an invitation to launch into a list of the government's failings but an opportunity to express what you enjoy most about their country. Cubans are known for their national pride and while they may have gripes about the economic or political situation they might not appreciate a foreigner lecturing them on the supposed ills of their country. It's just a question of respect.

When in doubt, listen rather than speak. If the person you are talking to wants to discuss the problems of the island, let them take the initiative. People's responses to their past history and present situation are both passionate and far more informed than you might think.

CARELESS TALK?

There might not be a spy on every corner listening to every conversation, but state security does monitor the population and especially suspected dissidents. By expressing or inviting strong critical opinions in conversation with Cubans you could be exposing them to state scrutiny. Ordinary tourists are highly unlikely to have a spy or "minder" keeping an eye on them, but people visiting Cuba for professional or business purposes—and particularly journalists—might well be under quiet surveillance. The wisest approach in conversation is to be politically discreet and noncommittal.

Let's Talk about Sex

Both men and women flirt with members of the opposite sex in shops, on the street, at the beach, in clubs; it's just part of daily life. Every other Cuban song is either a romantic ode to love or a down and dirty regaetton riddled with double meanings. Cubans are lighthearted but direct when discussing sex and will let you know if they like you.

Just be aware that Cuba is a tourist island and there are people who make a living from romantic liaisons with foreign visitors. Much is made of Cuba's *jineteras* (good-time girls), but there are the *jineteros* too, good-looking lotharios who work their magic on foreign ladies in return for financial favors. It's easy to get swept up in a swirl of emotion but keep in mind that for some Cubans sex is seen as a business, and marriage as a way to start a new life a foreign country.

Piropos—Cuban Chat-Up Lines

There's a lot of love in the air in Cuba. Both men and women will address each other—and tourists—as *mi amor* (my love), *mi corazon* (my heart), *mi cielo* (my heaven), or *mi reina/rey* (my queen/king), as just a normal part of saying hello on the street, or in shops.

Cubans are old-school Latin lovers when it comes to giving out flirtatious comments on the street. Known as *piropos*, these chat-up lines are meant to be humorous, and raise a smile that will lead to a conversation and, hopefully, some kind of hook up. They aren't very politically correct, and sound cheesy to foreign ears, but in reality they are a game that both Cuban men and women indulge in. It's hard otherwise to understand how anybody could expect success from lines like "*Si cocinas como caminas, me comiera hasta la raspa*" (If you cook like you walk, I'd scrape the pot). And while men will refer to women as *mami* (mommy) or a *manguita* (little mango), women will not hesitate in flirting with a man by calling him *papi* (daddy) or a *tremendo mangon* (lit. tremendous mango, hot guy). The key is to understand the game. You should neither swoon nor take offense just because a Cuban man spouts a few flowery phrases. He probably does it to everybody.

The best strategy is to do what the Cubans do, if you're not interested ignore the *piropos* and keep walking.

BREAKING OUT OF THE TOURIST BUBBLE

Most people come to Cuba as a package tourist staying at a resort on one of Cuba's amazing resort beaches like Varadero or Cayo Coco, exploring the museums and cultural highlights of a big city like Havana or Santiago de Cuba, or combining both. But there are many other ways to experience the country and get close to the real Cuba.

For US visitors general tourism and sand and sea holidays are still restricted, but the new rules brought in by the Obama administration in 2015 do allow for guided tours, volunteering, or study programs, which are a great way to meet Cubans and learn about the country.

If you plan to explore the country on your own, take dance classes, or study an instrument; a basic knowledge of Spanish will certainly help.

US Visitors

Organized tours are particularly important for US citizens, who don't have to apply for a license any more under the new rules, but do have to follow a full-time schedule of activities while in Cuba and justify their trip under one of the twelve exemptions, which include: visits to close relatives, professional research, academic programs for which students receive credits, participation in public performances or sports competitions, and journalistic, humanitarian, or religious activities.

Expat Groups

A networking group aimed at expats and foreign businesspeople spending time on the island is Internations, which has chapters all over the world and a Web site where members can make contact and exchange information. The Havana chapter organizes informal meet-ups where you can pick up tips on living in Cuba and explore the city with old hands.

Roads Less Traveled

It's more challenging—but by no means impossible, and potentially more rewarding—to go as an individual traveler.

To enter Cuba, citizens of most countries need only their passport, return tickets, and a thirty-day tourist card (not strictly speaking a visa, this is a separate paper that the Cuban immigration official stamps instead of your passport; you hand it in on departure).

You should also have evidence that you are staying in hotels, but in practice people often make hotel bookings (which appear on their tourist card) but stay with friends or in private houses (*casas particulares*).

If you have fairly confident Spanish, and are willing to spend time on making the arrangements, then getting to know a neighborhood in Havana or a smaller town like Baracoa, for example, by staying with families, shopping in markets, eating in *paladares*, and traveling in local buses rather than taxis, is a window into Cuban life you would never get in a resort.

Volunteering

If you want to do something useful during your stay, you can join one of the innumerable brigades and work–study tours organized by Cuba Solidarity groups and friendship associations abroad. Such organizations exist in over a hundred countries, including the US, so there will almost certainly be one near you. Brigades spend periods from a few weeks to a few months helping out in agriculture, construction, English teaching, or other activities. Most programs include educational visits and music and dancing. Church groups also organize trips for volunteers.

STAYING LONGER

Of course, the best way to get to know a country and its people is to live there, and work or study. Doing this in Cuba is not necessarily easy, and a lot of bureaucracy is involved—for instance, you will need an invitation and a visa specific to your purpose—but it is possible.

Cuba offers a variety of study opportunities: specialist institutes offer film and television, music, dance, and other performing arts, Afro–Cuban studies, and even medicine courses. Courses in various subjects are also available at the University of Havana. If you need to learn Spanish first, you can do that too. Short courses are available at Havana and Santiago universities and there are some language schools. If you are undertaking relevant research you can also arrange to visit Cuba for that purpose.

chapter **five**

THE CUBANS AT HOME

QUALITY OF LIFE

Things may be slowly changing in Cuba, but it still feels like you're living in a time warp, with its sit-up-and-beg Chinese bicycles, its shabby, romantic architecture, its much-mended '50s cars, and its laid-back *mañana* attitude (although a new entrepreneurial energy is definitely palpable on the street). But to many who have experienced the country, it is the spirit of the Cuban people that stands out—their ingenuity, their collective spirit, and insistence on getting by and enjoying the moment.

Cuba has never been a rich country, and now it is unequivocally poor in material resources. Nonetheless, according to the UN's Human Development Index, which uses criteria such as life expectancy, school enrolment, and literacy, as well as income, to measure a country's development, in 2014 Cuba ranked 44th in the world and second in Latin America and the Caribbean, after Chile.

Most Cubans still struggle to make ends meet each day. The word they use is *resolver*, to solve or resolve, a revealing word that suggests that making ends meet is a problem to be solved rather than an insuperable crisis.

Personal prosperity depends heavily on what currency you hold. People working in tourism consider themselves lucky since they have easy access to foreign currency or convertible pesos. State salaries paid in ordinary Cuban pesos are very low indeed, so even highly qualified professionals have other sources of income, licit and otherwise.

In mid-2014 the average wage in pesos for state workers was the equivalent in US dollars of about $20 a month for unskilled workers, rising to about $30 a month for skilled professionals. The extremely low wages paid to doctors and university professors often come as a shock to foreign visitors, especially situations where an Accident and Emergency surgeon might earn more driving a taxi or doing plumbing jobs for neighbors than from an official salary.

The Cuban state argues that Cubans might have low wages by foreign standards but they have access to free education at all levels, even for retirees, as well as health care, dental work, and medicines. Some essential foods are free or subsidized through the ration-book system. Rents are very low, in some cases free, and many Cubans now own their own homes, with minimal mortgage repayments to the state set at a maximum of 10 percent of the chief breadwinner's income. Gas, electricity, and telephone services are also subsidized.

Cubans might not have access to material goods such as high-end smartphones, video game consoles, new cars, flat screen TVs, and a whole host of other consumer products—unless they have relatives abroad bringing them over for them—but at the same time the general health, nutrition levels, life expectancy, and literacy rates of Cubans are ranked among the best in the world, and far above Cuba's Caribbean neighbors.

La Libreta

Rationing was introduced early in 1962 and has never ceased, though the range and quantities of products available on the ration book (*libreta*) fluctuate. The *libreta* covers staple foods and some shoes and clothes, particularly children's clothes. Newlyweds get a cake, three boxes of beer, and a special clothing ration. These products are bought at general stores called *bodegas,* always distinguishable by the lines outside them. Working families often send elderly members of the household to do the waiting in line for them.

TOWN AND COUNTRY

The Revolution changed rural life much more than urban. Fidel's experiences in the remote, impoverished Sierra Maestra confirmed his commitment to improving the lives of peasants,

producers of the country's main sources of wealth. The agrarian reform of 1960 gave land to the poorest rural people, sharecroppers and landless peasants, first in cooperatives, then in state farms, while small farmers were organized into the National Association of Small Farmers (ANAP). Since 1993, almost all state-owned agricultural land has been turned over to cooperatives, paid according to production.

Whatever the faults of collectivization, it did enable the government to improve the living conditions of peasants. A policy of "rural urbanization" narrowed the gap between town and country living standards by providing electricity, running water, education, and health care facilities to villages. Hundreds of new rural settlements were built: today multistory apartment blocks can be seen in the middle of the countryside, towering over tobacco or cane fields. Conversely,

the Special Period provided the impetus for some "urban ruralization." Vacant lots and city parks were used for intensive organic horticulture and town dwellers were encouraged to use their gardens to grow food.

HOUSING

The urban reform that accompanied the land reform in 1960 slashed rents and redirected rent revenues to the state instead of the landlords. Many homes of the rich were simply taken over by their servants when the owners fled. Most of these homes have become the property of their inhabitants. New homes can be bought from the state at a low-interest mortgage. In the 1960s and '70s, many apartment blocks were built by volunteer labor, the builders gaining the right to an apartment in the completed building.

However, dwellings can be very overcrowded, particularly in Havana's old central *barrios*, where

there is simply no room to expand as families grow. Private houses can now be bought and sold but the housing market is in its infancy and there is no real estate market in place. Informal real estate brokers operate by putting buyers and sellers in contact and earning a commission. Current regulations only allow Cuban nationals to own a main property and a vacation property, but with so many prospective million-dollar properties up for grabs, interest in Cuban real estate is high among Cuban exiles and foreign investors.

Most of the country is electrified, but the service is sporadic and unpredictable, and timetables for when water and electricity are available are unreliable. In remote parts of the country solar panels are being introduced. Power outages are the subject of many wry jokes; and it has been noticed that tourist resorts and hotels, the generators of national income, are often blazing with light when the rest of the country is in darkness.

HEALTH CARE

The health care system is generally agreed to be one of the Cuban Revolution's greatest achievements and to have raised Cubans' health indices to industrialized country levels. All Cubans get free health care by right.

The Revolution's first priorities were ensuring universal access to health care and eradicating the main infectious diseases by mass vaccination campaigns. The Family Doctor service was established in the 1980s to relieve the pressure on clinics and hospitals and to serve remote rural areas, each family doctor looking after roughly 120 families. Young doctors doing their rounds on horseback became a familiar sight among the mountain villages.

However, the health system has suffered from a severe shortage of resources because of the US embargo and the loss of Eastern European support. There is no shortage of trained personnel—indeed, Cuba sends doctors to other countries as a gesture of solidarity—or of health infrastructure, but a dire shortage of medicines. The government has therefore made a priority of preventive health care and is increasingly exploring the use of natural medicine, with a program of medicinal herb cultivation incorporated into organic agriculture. Meanwhile, more people are resorting to folk medicine as practiced by devotees of Santería.

As food shortages worsened during the early 1990s, international health organizations were predicting the return of nutrition-related diseases to Cuba, but the most serious results of this were averted by prioritizing protection of the most vulnerable people, children under five, and newborns and their mothers. Other diseases, such as typhoid fever and tuberculosis, also reemerged because water could not be purified in some areas. On the other hand, the Special Period had unintended positive effects on people's health, as they began to eat more vegetables and fruit and to take more exercise by walking and cycling. The absence of chemical inputs and automobile fumes has also improved food, soil, and air quality.

Hospitals also became shabby and under-equipped during the Special Period, and their way of making ends meet has unfortunately once again created a division between haves and have-nots, since the government has begun to take on paying patients from abroad to subsidize the state hospitals.

HIV/AIDS

According to UNAIDS, Cuba was one of the first countries to take AIDS seriously and devise a response combining prevention and care. However, the nature of that response is highly controversial. All Cuban AIDS patients are segregated in special sanatoriums, and HIV testing (using Cuban-produced kits) has become very general through a national screening program.

Draconian as this policy may seem, its results are incontrovertible. At 0.05 percent in 2003, Cuba's HIV infection rate is one of the lowest in the world. According to a foreign writer who visited one in 2002, the sanatoriums are pleasant, comfortable places where patients benefit from care and can have weekend passes and family visits. It is notable, too, that AIDS patients continue to receive their wages while they are in a sanatorium.

The US embargo deprived Cuba of antiretroviral drugs until 2001, when Cuban laboratories began manufacturing generic versions. Now Cuba is one of the few developing countries to offer all of its people with HIV/AIDS adequate medication.

Disability

The approach to disability is not as enlightened as the general approach to health care. Disabled people are guaranteed adequate health, rehabilitation, and employment services, but they are cared for in institutions rather than in the community, and employed in special factories. This approach is paternalistic but is perhaps the only affordable alternative to making the whole country disability-friendly. Disabled visitors will find few places accessible to wheelchairs or otherwise adapted for disabled people.

Mental health has also been addressed. Before 1959 there was only one public psychiatric hospital in Cuba. There are now three, in Havana, Camagüey, and Santiago de Cuba, and psychiatric units are attached to some general hospitals.

EDUCATION

Cuba's achievements in education are world-renowned. Education is free at all levels from preschool day care to university and lifelong learning, resulting in a well-educated and generally well-read workforce.

Following the thinking of both Marx and Martí, the education system combines schooling with practical experience in various ways, including taking city children to the countryside for six weeks a year.

There are also semi-boarding schools in the countryside where students combine classes with agricultural tasks during the week and go home on weekends. Critics of the Revolution see these simply as strategies for extracting cheap labor from young people, but they could equally be seen as ways of inculcating from an early age community spirit, consideration for others, and understanding of how the economy works.

THE CHANGING FAMILY

The Revolution has changed the way Cuban families live. Historically, extended families of three generations lived together, but this is less common nowadays because of housing pressures, especially in Havana, as well as short-lived marriages. Many Cubans have been through three marriages by the age of forty. People are having fewer children, and the number of households headed by women is increasing, partly because most emigrants since 1980 have been men.

The population is also aging, and the country has one of the highest proportions of senior citizens in Latin America, partly as a result of good health care for the elderly.

The Cuban diaspora has had serious impacts on the Cuban family; separation is painful whatever the motive for exile. Sometimes emigration divides families politically, but more often family members on both sides of the Florida Straits strive to preserve family unity, especially when people have emigrated for economic reasons. Many Cuban–Americans were angry in 2003 about President Bush's harsh measures cutting the frequency of permitted family visits to the island to once every three years.

THE DAILY ROUND

Cubans may seem laid back, but they lead extremely busy lives. The usual urban workday is roughly 8:30 a.m. to 5:30 p.m., Monday to Friday, with a one-hour lunch break; some workplaces also open on Saturday mornings. Many people make long and tedious journeys to work. In the countryside, the day regularly begins before dawn and finishes after dark.

The female members of the household do most of the domestic chores. The 1975 Family Code has

had very little impact on the traditional distribution of housework; taking the children to school or fetching the shopping is often the limit of a father's practical involvement in running the home. The austerity regime of the Special Period increased women's domestic labor, too, as more food had to prepared at home rather than bought, transportation between home and work took longer, and families could no longer afford to pay others to do laundry and cleaning.

In the evenings there are classes and cultural and other activities, but there is also time for just hanging out. Cubans visit each other frequently, and not necessarily with advance notice. Almost anything can be an occasion for a party at someone's home. On weekends during the hotter months, streams of buses take people to the beaches outside Havana. A growing number of Cubans now also go to church on Sundays, young people making up much of the congregation.

IN THE COMMUNITY

Cuba's tradition of night classes goes right back to the 1961 literacy campaign, when much of the teaching took place by the light of a storm lantern after the day's work in the fields or the home was over. Now Cubans of all ages take part in a vast array of community-based activities in the evenings, including night classes, music, dance, or theater group rehearsals, sports, and meetings.

Volunteer Work

Volunteer labor (*trabajo voluntario*) was introduced in 1962 as a temporary measure to bring in that year's sugar harvest and was later extended to other economic activities, including construction. It was constitutionally recognized in 1976 as a "forger of the communist conscience of our people." It is one of the clearest expressions of Che Guevara's conviction that moral rather than material incentives were a key principle of the new society. Several special days of mass volunteering were held in 2004 to celebrate the forty-fifth anniversary of the Revolution.

It is debated how truly voluntary *trabajo voluntario* is; although many people certainly do it out of commitment, others may be succumbing to social pressures from the government, the Party, or their workplace management and union branch, or undertaking volunteer work because it may increase their opportunities to get hold of certain scarce consumer items. People are paid their ordinary wage while doing volunteer work, so no one loses money. A pragmatic issue is the risk of using unqualified people in skilled trades such as construction.

THE CDRS

Membership of the Committees for the Defense of the Revolution is high—in the millions, according to pro-government sources—and, while not strictly speaking obligatory, reportedly necessary if you want to get ahead in the community or the Party. The organization was explicitly created for surveillance (see page 42), and was restructured at the end of the 1980s to respond to the needs of the Special Period. It still carries out crime-watching functions—in 2005 a "national surveillance exercise" was held to mark the forty-fifth anniversary of the organization's foundation—but it is not clear how far this extends to political espionage.

In other areas, such as coordinating disaster response, blood donation, vaccination and other public health campaigns, and recycling, the CDRs perform a vital service; but they have also been responsible for organizing threatening "rapid-response" gatherings outside the houses of dissidents.

chapter **six**

TIME OUT

Cubans enjoy their leisure time with just as much energy as they put into work. Making music, listening to it, and dancing to it are national obsessions. Movies and theatrical events are cheap and well attended. Sports like baseball, boxing, and athletics are practiced throughout the country, and international victories at the Olympics and the Pan-American Games are a huge source of national pride.

Cubans spend much of their free time outside, congregating with family and friends on street corners, in parks, and at the beach. One reason for this is that the tropical climate lends itself to outdoor life, but also because homes are often overcrowded and air

conditioning a luxury afforded by few. So Cubans head outside to eat ice-cream and street snacks, play chess or dominoes, and indulge in their favorite pastime—shooting the breeze.

FOOD

Few people visit Cuba for the food. A joke popular among Cuban exiles in Miami is that the first three victims of the Cuban Revolution were breakfast, lunch, and dinner. However, while it's true that most Cubans still rely on subsidized rations to get by each month, as the economy opens up to private enterprise and the quality of organically grown food at *agromercados*, or farmers markets, improves, more and more gastronomic experiences are opening up for Cubans and tourists.

For the average Cuban eating out is mostly confined to cheap treats like *coquitos* (sugary coconut sweets) and street snacks like pizzas and grilled sandwiches. One exception is the famous Coppelia ice-cream parlor, which has been serving up twenty-six flavors of subsidized *helado* since it opened in 1966 in Havana's hip Vedado district. There are now Coppelias in other cities too, and they are always worth a visit—if you don't mind

the lines—as they bring together Cubans from all walks of life.

State-run restaurants can be bland and the service indifferent, although some are housed in beautifully restored colonial buildings. In general they have improved with the tourist boom so it's worth checking around on Tripadvisor for tips.

Cheaper, and in many ways more interesting, are the *paladares*, family-run diners, often in private houses or apartments. Most are informal eateries serving home-cooked Cuban food to a good standard and in heaped portions. They used to be restricted to twelve diners but are now expanding into fully fledged restaurants. Always ask for a menu and check the prices before you order. If someone leads you to a *paladar*, be aware that their commission may be incorporated into your bill.

TIPPING

There is no formal requirement to tip. The usual restaurant tip is 10 percent in the same currency in which you have paid the bill. In *paladares* a gratuity is sometimes included in the bill, so check carefully and only pay it if you feel the service was adequate.

Elsewhere, Cuba lives from tips and everyone, from the doorman at the hotel to car park attendants and wandering musicians, will expect a tip. As in restaurants, this is at your discretion. A tour guide will expect around 2 CUC per person and taxi drivers 10 percent of the meter fare—but do not tip if you have negotiated a fare without a meter or are not happy with the ride.

Bills at restaurants and *paladares* alike are paid in CUC, although you can buy street snacks in pesos. Only the better restaurants and hotels will accept credit cards, so carry cash. Air-conditioning in formal hotel restaurants can be chilly, so take a light sweater. Few places will serve food after 10:00 p.m.

COMIDA CRIOLLA: POPULAR CUBAN DISHES

The basic Cuban trinity of fried pork, rice, and beans is tasty and filling but can get monotonous. At *paladares* you can get delicious home-cooked Cuban dishes at reasonable prices if you know what you are looking for.

Main Meals and Side Orders

Ajiaco—a one-pot stew of beef, corn, pumpkin or squash, plantains, and root vegetables like potatoes, yuca, and **boniato** (sweet potato). A deluxe *ajiaco* will come with beef, pork, and chicken, and some Cubans add beans. It's a stew made from whatever you have in the kitchen, so ask what's in it, or check out the pot.

Congrí—this is the classic Cuban dish of rice and beans cooked up together. Some Cubans differentiate between **moros y cristianos**, made with black beans and rice, and **congrí** or **congrís** made with kidney beans.

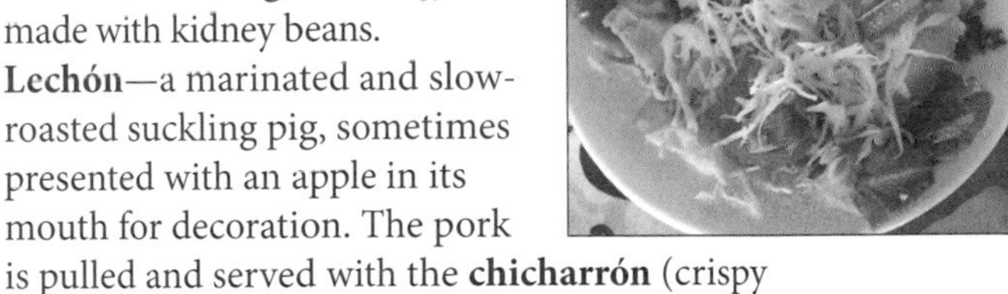

Lechón—a marinated and slow-roasted suckling pig, sometimes presented with an apple in its mouth for decoration. The pork is pulled and served with the **chicharrón** (crispy skin), *congrí*, yucca, and fried plantains.

Ropa Vieja—shredded beef or lamb prepared with a **sofrito,** a basic fried sauce of onions, garlic, green peppers, coriander, and tomatoes, and served with rice and beans.

Tamales—made from a cornmeal dough given an orange color with **bijol** (annatto) and mixed with chunks of fried pork or *chicharrón*, the *tamal* is wrapped in a corn husk and either boiled or placed on a barbecue. In Baracoa, they are made with mashed plantain dough and can be spicy.

Tostones—also known as **chatinos**, these are green plantain slices that are squashed and twice fried to crispy, golden perfection.

Yuca con Mojo—Fried yuca (also known as cassava), drizzled with an oil and garlic sauce.

Desserts

Tres Leches—A delicious combination of a sponge cake soaked in milk, condensensed milk, and layered in cream, *tres leches* (three milks)

is a sweet way to counter the savory assault of pork and beans.
Flan—Basically the same as creme caramel, this is a cold egg custard topped with caramel sauce.

Where's the Veg?

Cuba is a country where pork, rice, and beans is the norm, so it can be tricky for vegetarians looking for more than side-order combinations of vegetables. This is changing, however, and *paladares* are often happy to go off-menu and cook up an omelette, or add an avocado salad, to accompany a porkless plate of rice and beans.

There is now a wider range of tropical fruits and vegetables available from the *agromercados* and demand from tourists is gradually inspiring more *paladares* to take the plunge and create vegetarian dishes.

DRINKS

The fruit juices in Cuba aren't always as varied as in other Caribbean destinations but in big resorts and in the countryside you should find *jugos* (juices) of *naranja* (orange), *guayaba* (guava), *guanabana* (soursop), *piña* (pineapple), mamey, mango, and *sandia* (watermelon). Papaya is available as well but Cubans call it *fruta bomba* ("papaya" is used as a slang term for the vagina). In the countryside you can find stalls selling *guarapo*, a sweet, refreshing juice squeezed from sugar cane.

There are several Cuban *refrescos* (soft drinks), such as TropiCola, which goes into Cuba Libre cocktails, Najita, a Cuban orangeade, Jupiña, a fizzy pineapple, and some fizzy malt drinks.

Coffee is always strong and usually has sugar already added—ask for "*cafe sin azúcar*" if you don't take sugar, *cortado* for a dash of milk, and *café con leche* for a latte. Forget tea, although *manzanilla* (chamomile) tea is fairly common.

Cerveza (beer) is drunk very cold and at any time of the day. Popular pilsener style beers include Cristal and Bucanero. You can also get imported foreign beers like Heineken and Corona in resorts and clubs in Havana. Cuba does produce its own wine under the Soroa label, but imported wine is better.

COCKTAILS WITH HISTORY

Cuba is internationally famous for its rum and rum-based cocktails, such as the *mojito* (white rum, lime juice, sugar, and a sprig of mint), the *daiquiri* (white rum, lime juice and sugar without ice), and the *Cuba libre* (white rum poured over ice, coca cola, and a squeeze of lime).

Perhaps the most famous place to drink *mojitos* in Havana is the Bodeguita del Medio, once the hangout of US novelist Ernest "Papa" Hemingway, among other famous drinkers.

Hemingway's favorite haunt in Havana was the Floridita, now a rather plush affair, where he created his own daiquiri cocktail, *El Papa Doble*—a double shot of white rum, with lime and grapefruit juice, blended with ice and served frappe, like a slush puppy.

In keeping with his tough guy image, Hemingway drank his *daiquiris* without sugar. The *Cuba libre* (Free Cuba) goes back to the years after 1900, when—rather ironically—the independence motto was used as a toast by the US Marines who brought Coca Cola to the island.

Cuban rums like Havana Club are excellent quality and cheap, starting at around 3 to 5 CUC for the Silver Dry white rum up to 12 CUC for the seven-year-old Añejo 7 años. Other brands such as Santero, Mulata, Santiago, Caney, and Varadero are even cheaper and it's well worth putting in some research at the bar to find the best *mojito* rum in Cuba.

THE ARTS

The Cuban Revolution not only focused on education and healthcare, it also invested heavily in culture, both folk culture and music and high culture such as ballet, classical music, and the fine arts. Museums and art galleries were opened, orchestras, dance academies, theater groups, and art schools were created, and a national film industry was born, making culture accessible to all Cubans for the first time.

Casas de la Cultura are cultural centers found in all most towns and cities where people can take evening classes, join a choir or a municipal band, hear concerts, and watch movies, The Casa de las Américas, founded in 1960, has grown into one of Latin America's most prestigious cultural institutions, awarding annual literary, musical, and artistic prizes and holding conferences, exhibitions, and concerts. There are also national institutes for writers, artists, and the cinema.

Creative artists in Cuba are employed by the state; they don't have to wait tables or work in shops to fund their art, waiting for the "big break," though teaching may be an integral part of their jobs.

Music

When US guitarist Ry Cooder and Cuban bandleader Juan de Marcos González recorded an album in Havana with a group of veteran musicians in 1996, they not only created the Buena Vista Social Club, they also reminded the world of the wonders of Afro-Cuban musical styles like the *son*,

rumba, *mambo*, and *danzon*. The Grammy-winning album went on to sell 12.5 million copies, and a follow-up documentary movie by Wim Wenders sparked a huge interest in Cuban music around the world, which in turn has boosted tourism.

Music is everywhere in Cuba, from the drumming at Santeria rituals, to the *conga* groups of carnival, and the romantic *boleros* and *mambos* of the golden age of the 1940s and 1950s. There are numerous styles of Latin jazz, the reflective acoustic songs of the Nueva Trova, drum-heavy *rumba*, fusion forms like *timba*, the country guitar of *guajira* music, and contemporary urban sounds like rap and reggaeton.

While artists like Benny Moré, Dámaso Pérez Prado, and Arsenio Rodriguez led the mambo boom of the 1940s and the Buena Vista did the same in the 1990s, the latest attack on the US charts is coming from urban groups like Gente de Zona.

For an immersion in the old school glamor of pre-revolution Havana head to the Tropicana nightclub in Havana. For something less formal search out a *cumbancha* (street party), or live music in a café or bar. But the best way to experience music in Cuba is at a local *Casa de la Trova*, especially in Santiago, which has a whole street dedicated to music, Calle Heredia.

The classical music scene is just as vibrant, with orchestras and chamber groups active all over the country and top venues in Havana the Teatro Amadeo Roldán and the Basilica de San Francisco de Asís.

Cuba also has a full calendar of international music festivals to suit all tastes.

Dance

Cubans seem to have dance in their DNA. There are two principal national dance companies—the Conjunto Folklórico Nacional de Cuba, founded in 1962 to celebrate traditional and Afro-Cuban dance, and the Ballet Nacional de Cuba, founded in 1948 by the prima ballerina assoluta Alicia Alonso. There is also the Ballet de Camagüey, and there are several modern dance companies.

Among many opportunities to see dance performances, the Conjunto Folklórico Nacional

gives a *rumba* performance every Saturday in Havana, while the Ballet Nacional de Cuba performs year-round at the Gran Teatro de La Habana and organizes an annual ballet festival.

One of the most famous male dancers in the world today is Carlos Acosta, who has danced with the Houston Ballet, the Bolshoi in Russia, and became principal dancer at the Royal Ballet in London. The youngest of eleven children, Acosta made it out of the back streets of Havana after training with Alicia Alonso's Escuela Nacional Cubana de Ballet. His biography *No Way Home* became an instant bestseller, and his novel *Pig's Foot* vividly conjures up Cuba and its tumultuous history.

Cinema and Theater

Cuban cinema is another of the glories of the Revolution, made possible by the founding in 1959 of the Cuban film institute ICAIC. The 1960s was a golden age in Cuban cinema, culminating in 1968, the year of Tomás Gutiérrez Alea's *Memorias del Subdesarrollo* (*Memories of Underdevelopment*) and Humberto Solás' *Lucia*; but world-class films continue to appear despite economic constraints.

One of the most popular movies of recent years is director Alejandro Brugués' irreverent zombie comedy *Juan of the Dead*, a satire that pokes fun at the daily hardships facing Cubans while raising a laugh. Shot using digital effects for US $3 million, the movie is part of a new wave of privately funded films and has had some success abroad.

The main event for film buffs is the annual Festival Internacional del Cine Latinoamericano held in Havana in December.

Cuba's colorful screenprinted film posters make excellent souvenirs. You can buy them at a store in front of ICAIC in Vedado.

Theater

Before the Revolution Cuba had fewer than fifteen theaters, but now there are over sixty, and Havana hosts a biennial international theater festival. All the main cities offer mainstream and experimental productions. Teatro Cabildo in Santiago and El Público in Havana have their own permanent theaters. Teatro Escambray, founded in 1968 as a community-based

theater in the rural zones of the Escambray Mountains, is still active in both performance and teaching.

Visual Arts

Many of the painters who define the national artistic idiom, such as Wifredo Lam (1902–82) and René Portocarrero (1912–85), predate the Revolution but embraced it. After 1959 a program of art education was developed and the National School of Art and the Institute for Advanced Art Studies were founded. Castro ignored fine art, but never actually restricted it, which meant that it was not reduced to political propaganda. Graphic arts, however, became an essential channel for revolutionary messages, and tremendous creativity went into posters and murals.

Now the government enthusiastically promotes Cuban art. Galleries are state-run, and works may be bought through them. Recent generations of Cuban artists, including Manuel Mendive, whose work is based on Yoruba myths and traditions, and Flora Fong, have achieved international recognition. Exhibitions such as the Havana Biennial, held in November in odd-numbered years, help to promote young artists.

For gallery events, consult the free publication *Arte en La Habana*. Some of Cuba's best works from the contemporary and earlier periods can be viewed in Havana's Museo Nacional de Bellas Artes.

Literature and Books

Questions of national identity and social problems have always featured in Cuban literature, and the works of Independence hero José Martí are a classic example. Slavery was a favorite subject of nineteenth-century novels and in the post-revolutionary period novelists like Alejo Carpentier used "magical realism" to explore the past and tap into the Latin American experience. Modern genres such as crime fiction are now very popular, and the best-known contemporary Cuban writer, both in Cuba and abroad, is Leonardo Padura, whose Havana Quartet series of books about Detective Mario Conde have been translated into twelve languages.

Books are still a big deal in Cuba and Havana's International Book Fair, held in January or February, attracts a large literary crowd.

CENSORSHIP

The Revolution promoted intellectual freedom and artistic creativity at first, but a siege mentality set in after the Bay of Pigs, with strict boundaries on freedom of expression. In his 1961 "Speech to the Intellectuals," Fidel Castro said: "Within the Revolution, everything, against the Revolution nothing. We don't tell anyone what to write about . . . but we will always judge their literary work through the prism of the Revolution." The Soviet-influenced 1970s was the toughest decade for intellectual freedom, but there has been a marked relaxation in prejudice and censorship since the 1990s, witnessed by the success of authors such as Leonardo Padura.

SPORTS AND OUTDOOR ACTIVITIES

Although professional sporting activity was abolished after the Revolution, large resources have been invested in amateur sports, which are seen as a source of national pride and an advertisement for the Revolution.

Baseball (*beisbol*) and boxing are the most popular sports. Baseball arrived from the USA in the 1860s and is now, ironically, the national game. Cuba won the first-ever Olympic gold in baseball at the 1992 Barcelona games. Matches are well worth attending, even if just for the atmosphere. The larger stadiums have reserved seating areas for foreigners, but it's more fun to mingle with the Cuban spectators.

Cuba has won several Olympic boxing titles, Teófilo Stevenson being especially revered. Two athletic Olympians are Alberto Juantorena and María Colón. All were at their peak in the 1970s.

Other major sports played in Cuba include volleyball, basketball, and, increasingly, football. In rural areas cockfighting is common but illegal. Chess games are a common sight on front stoops and in parks, and sultry evenings often resound to the clack of dominoes and the clink of rum-filled glasses.

Mass tourism has opened the floodgates for outdoor pursuits. Diving, surfing, and game fishing are favorites. The waters off the Isla de la Juventud provide one of the world's great diving sites. Most holiday villages have tennis courts, and some their own golf courses. Cycling, walking, and trekking on horseback are growing activities. The Sierra Maestra and the Topes de Collantes, near Trinidad, are beautiful hiking areas. Hikes to the mountaintops require a guide, but unguided low-level trails are being developed, as are specialist ecotourism programs for bird-watchers, botanists, and cavers.

SHOPPING FOR PLEASURE

Cuba is not a consumer society and the range of goods in shops is severely restricted by state control of the economy. Cubans still use ration cards for food and some other items, but in recent years there has been a growth in department stores, supermarkets, and small shopping malls that sell goods in CUC to foreign visitors and Cubans with access to tourist currency.

Some fine art is sold at galleries, but you need a special license and certificate of authenticity to take artworks out of the country. The secondhand book market in Havana's Plaza de Armas is an excellent place to pick up out-of-print Cuban classics.

CUBAN CIGARS

Cuba produces the best cigars in the world and in a dizzying number of brands, varieties, and sizes. Top names include Monte Cristo, Partagas, Hoyo De Monterrey, Cohiba, and Romeo y Julieta, the cigars favored by Sir Winston Churchill. A highly labor-intensive crop, tobacco is grown mostly on small farms, principally in Vuelta Abajo and Semi-Vuelta in Pinar del Río Province, Viñales, and in parts of central Cuba. Avoid the street hustlers selling

fake cigars and head to one of the state-run Casas del Habano. Make sure the box bears the label *hecho in Cuba totalmente a mano* (totally handmade in Cuba), the official government seal, and the "Habanos" band. If not, the cigars are not genuine. Cigars labeled "Bauza" do not meet the required standards but are still of good quality.

PLACES TO VISIT

Historic Havana

One of the most vibrant, intriguing, and unforgettable cities in the Caribbean, Havana is a bucket list destination that actually manages to live up to, or exceed, expectations. It's definitely a city of faded glamor, with crumbling mansions, and rusting Chevys cruising potholed streets past peeling murals bearing

revolutionary slogans. Yet Havana contains some of the finest colonial architecture in the Americas, and has been undergoing a major restoration program since it was designated a UNESCO World Heritage Site in 1982. Some of the best buildings have been converted into museums, and you could easily take a week to explore the city. But Havana's main appeal is out on the streets, mingling with the Habaneros a they hang out on the Malecón, eat ice-cream at Coppelia's, and crawl from bar to bar, the sound of Cuban *son* the soundtrack of the city.

Santiago de Cuba

Cuba's second-largest city, with a population of 443,000, is in the far east of the island. Founded in 1515 by Diego Velazquez, it is a vibrant melting pot of cultures and architectural styles, but it is best known internationally for music, which today pours from every doorway, day and night. Santiago is the home of *son*, the distinctive Afro–Cuban musical style, and its Casa de la Trova is the best place to start any exploration of the city.

Colonial Trinidad

Nestling under the Escambray Mountains, Trinidad has the reputation of being Cuba's most "unspoiled" town. UNESCO placed it on the World Heritage list in 1988, which may explain the impression it gives of being preserved in aspic, with its pretty pastel-colored houses and narrow cobbled streets made of the very stones used as ballast in the slave and sugar ships.

Revolutionary Cuba

Those wanting to immerse themselves in the revolutionary history of the island usually start in Havana with a tour of the Museum of the Revolution and include trips to the Moncada barracks (Cuartel de Moncada) in Santiago, the Che Guevara Memorial (Monumento Ernesto Che Guevara) in Santa Clara, and the Bay of Pigs (Playa Girón). You can also take guided trips up into the Sierra Maestra mountains to get an idea of what life was like for the bearded revolutionaries as they fought the Batista regime.

A Paradise for Anglers

The largest island in the Caribbean, surrounded by reefs, saltwater flats, and mangroves, Cuba offers anglers and divers one of the richest marine environments in the world, with fly fishing for fast and elusive bonefish, or the physical battle of landing tarpon or marlin. Around the coast, you can fish for yellow tail snapper, red snapper, and bonito from an inner tube like a local, or take a boat from Cayo Santa Maria on the north coast to fish for acrobatic tarpon reaching 8 feet (2.5 meters) in length. The highlight of Cuba's fishing year is the Ernest Hemingway International Billfishing Tournament, held in May or June at the Marina Hemingway since 1950, attracting anglers from some thirty countries, including the USA. Another highlight is the Jardines del Rey Big Game Trolling tournament held in Cayo Guillermo in October.

Cycling Tours

With so few cars on the roads cycling is a popular tourism option, with short routes from Havana past picturesque tobacco fields in Viñales or Pinar del Río, or week-long expeditions all the way to Santiago de Cuba. You can either join a specialist tour, where bikes and guides are provided, or bring your own bike and travel independently. Bring your own helmet and a sturdy bike lock as well, as a good bike is worth a fortune in Cuba. In some resorts you can rent out the steel-frame Chinese bikes that Cubans use, but they are only suited to day trips around towns and resorts.

Wildlife Watching

It may be the largest island in the Caribbean, but the most sought after endemic species in Cuba are very small indeed. The minuscule bee hummingbird, or *zunzuncito* (*Mellisuga helenae*), is the smallest bird in the world. It can be found flittering about in many areas, including the *mogotes* around Viñales, the Sierra de Anafe, Guanahacabibes Peninsula, the Zapata swamp, and on Isla de la Juventud.

In the Humboldt National Park, you need a keen eye to spot the Mount Iberia frog (*Eleutherodactylus iberia*), a dwarf species that was only discovered in 1996 on the forested slopes of Mount Iberia and for a while was ranked a Guinness World Record holder as the world's smallest frog (it's now third). Only 3/8 of an inch (10mm) long, this cute critter easily fits on an adult finger nail.

Cuba is a magnet for bat lovers as the island is home to twenty-seven species, the most in the Caribbean. The butterfly bat is one of the world's smallest, weighing less than an ounce. Other endemics include a large rodent called a Cuban hutia (*Capromys pilorides*), and the Cuban crocodile (*Crocodylus rhombifer*), which can reach a length of 11 ft (3.5 m) and weigh in at 474 lb (215 kg).

chapter **seven**

TRAVEL, HEALTH, & SAFETY

GETTING AROUND

Cuba is a bigger island than most people imagine and getting around, even on roads devoid of any major traffic, can be time consuming. The quickest way to travel is by air, and there are regular internal flights linking Cuba's main airports with the capital, Havana, and second city, Santiago de Cuba. Unlike the rest of the Caribbean, Cuba also has a rail network, which can be fun to explore, but slow.

For many people, the first experience of Cuba is a taxi ride in a Buick or Chevy, and classic cars from the '50s have become an iconic image of the island. But Cubans run vintage cars out of necessity, not choice. Only some 5 percent of Cubans currently own their own cars, despite new rules in 2011 allowing people to buy and sell them. Until salaries improve markedly that situation looks unlikely to change, although the recent thaw in US–Cuba relations could bring badly needed spares to the island.

Air Travel

Cuba receives flights from all over the world—including charter flights from the US—and has international airports serving the cities of Havana,

Santiago, Holguín, Santa Clara, Camagüey, Manzanillo, and Cienfuegos, as well as the beach resorts of Varadero, Cayo Coco, and Cayo Largo del Sur. The busiest airport by far is Havana's José Martí International Airport, which receives some 4 million passengers a year, and is the main hub for internal flights. The resort of Varadero comes second with about 25 percent of Cuba's international air traffic.

Although internal flights save valuable vacation time when compared to buses and trains, there are safety questions over Cuba's ageing fleet of Russian Antonovs. The situation is improving as local airlines switch over to modern planes like the French–Italian ATR. Buy tickets at hotel tour desks and travel agencies rather than at airline offices, which are invariably chaotic.

Trains

The state railway company is called Ferrocarriles de Cuba and serves Havana and the provincial capitals. If you are not in a hurry, the train is a good option. It is safe and comfortable, and getting a ticket is normally easy. Always arrive at the station with time to spare as you may need to get your ticket restamped or your passport checked before you can travel.

Foreigners can book in advance at the larger hotels or through Ferrotur offices or the LADIS agency, and must pay in CUC.

In smaller towns and for local trains you will have to join the line at the ticket office at least two hours before the train is due. Boarding without a ticket attracts a 100 percent surcharge.

Interprovincial trains usually depart from the main Estación Central in Havana, but while it is undergoing renovation trains are leaving from the nearby La Coubre station.

There is a "fast" train joining Havana and Santiago de Cuba that is known as the "Tren Francés" (the French train) because it uses old Trans–Europe Express carriages bought from France in 2001. It has non-smoking cars, a buffet service, Arctic air-conditioning, and takes about 12 to 15 hours to travel the 531 miles (860 km) between Havana and Santiago de Cuba, stopping at Santa Clara and Camagüey. As with all long-distance travel in Cuba, make sure to bring your own toilet roll.

Most trains are classed as *regular* (ordinary). They are slower and don't have non-smoking cars. There is no air-conditioning but the windows can be opened. Not all have a buffet service. Trains classed as *lecheros* (milk trains) are really basic, stopping at every tiny hamlet.

The astonishingly slow "Hershey train"—the tracks were laid by the American chocolate firm—is

Cuba's only electric train and runs between Havana and Matanzas. Rolling through lush greenery past sugar mills makes for a charming day out. Pack snacks and bottled water and take the bus back!

Buses

Most tourists travel around on tour buses, which can be arranged at short notice from resorts, hotels, and guesthouses, and are comfortable, but pricier than taking local buses.

The state-run company Viazul offers a reliable, punctual, and comfortable service to major towns and tourist spots on buses with toilets and glacial air-conditioning. The Viazul terminal in Havana is a taxi journey from the city center. Although refreshment stops are frequent, it's advisable to take your own food. Reboard promptly, or you may lose your seat.

Another state-run company aimed at local travelers, Astro, serves virtually every town in the country, but many services run only on alternate days and some leave in the middle of the night.

Travel on local buses is very cheap (payable in pesos), but you can't make reservations. Local services are often run by provincial enterprises and you may have to change services at provincial boundaries and buy a fresh ticket. Arrive early at bus stations. You'll be put on a list or given a number. Don't wander off, or you could miss your turn. Be alert for scams, such as being told the wrong departure time for your bus, so that you miss it and the ticket seller then tries to sell you a seat in a private taxi.

Trucks

For the adventurous, open trucks (*camiones*), minimally converted for passengers, are an uncomfortable but cheap and relatively fast way to travel between provinces. There are departure points in every city, and the trucks run to a (fairly loose) schedule. Payment, made as you board, is a fraction of the bus fare. An excellent way of meeting local people!

Long-distance Taxis

Long-distance taxis can be found at train stations and interprovincial bus stations. They have fixed routes (often painted on the hoods) and leave only when they are full, which can mean a wait. However, they do offer an alternative to the long lines at bus stations. State-owned CUC taxis (*colectivos*) are faster and sometimes cheaper than buses. State-owned peso taxis (*máquinas*) are not allowed to take foreigners, but often do. Private taxis (*particulares*) are cheaper than most other taxis. Some are metered but you will need to negotiate a price before departure.

Car Rental

To rent a car you will need to show a valid driver's license or an international license, be over the age of twenty-one with a valid passport, and leave a deposit in cash or an imprint of a non-US credit card. No international car companies operate in Cuba but the usual car rental procedures apply with the national ones. Check the car for any damage pre-departure, and beware of additional charges that suddenly appear on your bill when you return it. It's advisable to take out optional insurance for rental cars to cover accidents and theft. There is a penalty charge if you lose your car rental contract, and if you are involved in an accident you must get a copy of the police report (*denuncia*) and hand it to the car rental company to be eligible for the insurance coverage.

Gasoline is available at Servi-Cupet stations (*servicentros*, commonly known as *servis*). There are two grades, *especial* and *regular*, but foreigners will only be served *especial*. *Servis* often form the central hub of small towns and are open twenty-four hours a day. Outside the towns there are very few gas stations and Cubans will travel with gas cans in the trunk. A good road map is essential. The *Mapa Turístico de Cuba*, although not the best, indicates the locations of gas stations.

In response to the transportation crisis, Cubans have taken to organized hitchhiking. At major junctions away from city centers, traffic lights, and rail crossings, people known as *amarillos* stop vehicles to find out their destinations. This is legal, and can be useful to foreign drivers unfamiliar with an area. It is best for foreign hitchhikers to travel in pairs.

Road conditions are bad in general, and night driving is particularly hazardous due to non-existent lighting or cat's eyes, and the likelihood of running into dogs, livestock, horses, bicycles without lights, or even trains.

Rules of the Road

Cubans officially drive on the right, but don't always adhere to this on country roads; in any case potholes can make it impossible. Speed limits are 31 mph (50 kmph) in urban areas, 56 mph (90 kmph) on open roads, with some areas restricted to 37 mph (60 kmph), and 62–75 mph (100–120 kmph) on highways (*autopistas*).

Cubans drive as fast as their vehicles will allow, which, fortunately, is not very fast. There are on-the-spot fines for speeding, and speed traps are common on the *autopista*. There is no law on seat belts, which are generally fitted only in officially rented cars. The official blood/alcohol limit is 80 mg/100 ml, and there is a hefty on-the-spot fine for foreigners caught drink driving.

If you encounter a *punta de control* (police checkpoint), you must stop. Sentry boxes are installed at most major intersections. A sign saying "*pare*," a red upside-down triangle inside a red circle, means "Stop," not "Give way," which is "*ceda el paso*" in a red upside-down triangle on a yellow background. Standard international road signs are in use, but sporadically, and directional signs are often obscure or missing.

If you are involved in an accident, do not move your vehicle, or allow any other vehicle involved to be moved. Take all relevant details and call the transit police. If someone is seriously injured or killed you must contact your embassy. If you are held responsible for the accident, the police can confiscate your passport so that you cannot leave the country.

Parking is generally a free-for-all, but you must park on the left in one-way streets, and your car will be removed if you park in zones marked *Zona Oficial*. Most tourist hotels provide parking; if you do park on the street overnight, it's best to pay the hotel doorman to keep an eye on the car.

Ferries

Ferries and hydrofoils serve the Isla de la Juventud from Suridero de Batabano on the southern coast. Cubanacán also runs brand-new catamarans that can convey up to 400 passengers between Varadero and Havana. Small ferries connect the coast north of Pinar del Río with Cayo Levisa.

IN TOWNS AND RESORTS

Cuban cities are mostly laid out on a grid pattern. Parallel streets (*calles*) are crossed by avenues (*avenidas*). In some cities streets and avenues are named and in others numbered or lettered, usually in a regular pattern that makes it easy to navigate. Every city has a central *plaza* or *parque*. Some streets retain their pre-revolutionary names alongside the new ones introduced in 1959, which can be confusing. When asked, locals usually overestimate the time you need to walk anywhere.

Taxis

The easiest way of getting around cities is by taxi, with taxis for foreigners (charging in CUC) and taxis for Cubans in pesos. Taxi stands are in front of all major hotels, at airports, and at strategic points around cities, but taxis can also be ordered by phone or hailed in the street. Most taxis are metered, the money going to the state, but many drivers will offer the foreigner a flat, off-meter rate that the driver then pockets. Insist on the meter unless you know the fare.

Social Media Moments

For a novelty ride that will look good on Facebook or Instagram, opt for a coco-taxi—an egg-shaped three-seater scooter—or one of the many bicycle rickshaws, or a horse-drawn cabs that offer pricey trips round town.

Buses

City buses, known as *guaguas*, are invariably overcrowded and hot and may be targeted by pickpockets. They ply fixed routes but you will need to know your way around to use them confidently. Inventive responses to the fuel crisis are the *ciclobus*, which carries passengers together with their bicycles. The large, unwieldy semitrailer buses nicknamed *camellos* (camels) no longer haul passengers around Havana but can still be found elsewhere. Urban bus fares in Cuba are less than a peso. *Lanchas* are waterbuses that serve the communities around the bay areas of Havana, Santiago, and Cienfuegos.

Bicycles and Motorcycles

The Special Period saw a boom in bicycles. A million Phoenix, Flying Pigeon, and Forever bikes were imported from China, and they now outnumber cars 20:1. There are bike lanes and *poncheras* (puncture repair shops) everywhere and with typical ingenuity Cubans have adapted bicycles to carry passengers, *bicitaxis*, and also to move merchandise.

Bicycle rental is rare, available mainly in the Havana area or in tourist centers, but you should bring your own helmet, padlock, and padded shorts if you plan any serious cycling in Cuba.

There are few motorcycle facilities, but scooters and mopeds can be rented in many resorts.

WHERE TO STAY

Before the Revolution, Cuba had some of the finest hotels in the world. It was a playground for Hollywood stars and the international jet set, and casinos, clubs, and hotels like the Hotel Nacional de Cuba and the Havana Riviera were built and run

by top mafia mobsters like Santos Traficante Jr. and Meyer Lansky.

Thanks to a new wave of foreign investment in the 1990s, Cuba embarked on a major program of tourism construction, creating resorts like Varadero, near Havana, and Cayo Coco and Cayo Guillermo out on the stunning Jardines del Rey archipelago. Spain's Melia Hotel Chain opened its first hotel in Varadero in 1990 and now manages twenty-seven properties on the island, making it Cuba's most important foreign tourism partner.

Many of the old hotels and beautiful colonial buildings are being refurbished to international standards. The high priority put on international tourism as an income generator makes water and electricity outages less frequent in tourist establishments than elsewhere.

Hotels are classified by the international star system, though standards can vary widely, especially in some of the older resort hotels. Peak seasons are December to March and July to August. Finding a hotel room is becoming harder with the recent surge in interest so book well ahead, even out of season. It is also worth checking if breakfast is included in the price before booking. Cubans are no longer excluded from resorts, so they are not the tourist-only bubbles they were in the past.

A good alternative to a hotel is to stay in a *casa particular* (privately run guesthouse), identified with a sticker showing two blue triangles and the inscription *Arrendador Inscripto*. It is legal to stay with a Cuban family as long as they are registered taxpayers. If you stay at an illegal residence, the family could face a fine.

Official campsites are springing up all over Cuba, consisting of cabins rather than tents, typically with a restaurant and swimming pool. Sleeping on beaches or putting up a tent in a field is illegal.

HEALTH

Vaccinations are not required by Cuban Immigration, but protection against hepatitis A, typhoid, polio, and tetanus is recommended. If you have come from or been through areas infected by yellow fever and cholera you should bring a vaccination certificate.

Cuba has an excellent health service, but the Cuban authorities insist all visitors have adequate health insurance as health care is not free for visitors treated in international clinics or public hospitals.

MEDICAL TOURISM

With its well-trained doctors and its documented successes in tackling vitiligo, HIV infection, and cancer, Cuba has built up an enviable reputation for its health facilities. The result has been a boom in medical tourism as foreigners travel to the island to undergo specific procedures. Eye surgery, physiotherapy, and cosmetic treatments like nose jobs and liposuction are all popular and cheaper than in Canada, Europe, or the US. Drug and alcohol rehabilitation programs attract famous clients like the Argentinian footballer Diego Maradona. Some health facilities are run like five-star resorts, raising fears that a two-tier health system is developing, although it is hoped that money from medical tourism will help fund the state sector.

In Havana, the Ciro García Central Clinic caters to foreigners only and the Hermanos Ameijeiras hospital has special floors for foreigners. Servimed, a state-run but for-profit health system for foreigners, has many centers around Cuba. Foreigners are often allowed to go ahead of others in regular health facilities but will be expected to pay in cash. International hotels have a doctor on call and many have a pharmacy.

Pharmacies are generally poorly stocked—bring your own medicine, sunscreen, and cosmetics. International pharmacies and supermarkets are better stocked with basics but are not in every town. Opening times are: *turno regular* 8:00 a.m. to 5:00 p.m. daily, *turno especial* 8:00 a.m. to 10:30 p.m., and *turno permanente*, open 24 hours a day.

Common Ailments

The most common ailment to strike visitors is travelers' diarrhea, and this should clear up within two to three days. If it persists—and is combined with fever—it's worth going to a clinic for a test. There have been problems with giardia, a protozoan parasite typically transmitted through infected water, so stick to bottled or boiled water, and when buying food in the street stick to things that are cooked in front of you.

Public toilets can be hard to find and are not always in perfect condition so make sure to pack a few extra toilet rolls and wet wipes, as they are expensive in Cuba.

It's important to protect yourself against sunburn and heatstroke with a high factor cream applied before going into the sun, and hydrating properly with lots of water. Even when there's a breeze on the beach, or on overcast days, you can burn in a few hours without sun cream. Despite the heat, some people will pick up a summer cold, perhaps from the contrast between sweltering street heat and icy air-conditioning in some restaurants.

Insects are more of a nuisance than a hazard. You will need to come to terms with sharing your room with various creepy-crawlies, especially in cheap hotels. Mosquitoes are the main menace, and although they do not carry malaria, they can make your evenings and nights a misery. Bring your own insect repellent and, if you plan to camp, a mosquito net.

Passive smoking in restaurants, hotels, and public transportation is hard to avoid. Cuba is beginning to take measures against smoking, but very few restaurants have non-smoking areas and any "no smoking" signs are blithely ignored.

CRIME AND SAFETY

Cuba has very low levels of violent crime and is considered much safer for tourists than its Caribbean and Latin American neighbors. However, street hustlers (*jineteros/as*) and their various scams to separate tourists from their cash can be a nuisance at times, and visitors should guard against pickpocketing and petty theft in tourist areas in cities and on popular beaches.

Hustlers will try to sell you fake cigars (or marijuana, or sex), or to earn commission by taking you to a *paladar* to eat or a *casa particular* to spend the night (which all adds to the final bill), but they will soon disappear if you threaten to call the police.

Havana is a relatively safe city to walk around, even at night, but avoid walking alone and stick to well-lit streets where possible. If you are robbed report it to the Policía Nacional Revolucionaria (PNR), who wear light blue shirts and blue trousers. There is also a special police corps to protect tourists from pickpockets in tourist spots. They wear a dark blue uniform. Not all police speak English.

For insurance purposes you should insist on a stamped, dated police report (*denuncia*) outlining the details of what happened and the items stolen. In Havana the police will have more experience of dealing with tourists but be prepared for a long wait at the police station.

If you are a victim of crime, you are unlikely to be harmed as violence against tourists is rare. Take all the usual precautions, including leaving valuables in a hotel safety deposit box (*caja de seguridad*) and carrying only what you are prepared to lose.

STAY WITHIN THE LAW

It is illegal to take photographs of anything with a military connection, especially at airports, and even from an aircraft in Cuban airspace. Taking photographs of a political protest could also result in problems.

There is zero tolerance for drugs, and penalties for marijuana and cocaine possession are strictly enforced. Drug smuggling carries heavy penalties.

Possessing or producing pornography is severely penalized in Cuba and tourists should be aware that anyone convicted of corrupting a minor (under sixteen) or sex-trafficking offenses will face a lengthy prison sentence.

chapter **eight**

BUSINESS BRIEFING

THE ECONOMIC CLIMATE

Cuba is a one-party state with a centrally controlled economy. Outside the small-scale private sector that individual Cubans are allowed to run, all business done on the island needs the approval of the state or a partnership with one of the state monopolies, many of them run directly by GAESA, a conglomerate of companies controlled the Revolutionary Armed Forces of Cuba. Over 80 percent of the workforce is employed by the state, about 25 percent is self-employed, and unemployment runs at about 5 percent, according to Cuban government statistics.

Cuba has a world-class pharmaceutical and biotechnology industry, important reserves of nickel and cobalt, and a thriving tourism sector. Companies from China, Canada, Venezuela, Spain, Italy, France, the United Kingdom, and Mexico all have investments in Cuba, in sectors including energy, financial services, mining, manufacturing, IT, and tourism, and the government is keen for further investment in these and other sectors.

Cuba now trades with many countries, and the historic reestablishment of political relations with the US in 2015 has opened the door to increased trade with the US, particularly in food, agriculture, and telecommunications. However, the US embargo remains in place and many restrictions still apply. At the heart of the government's economic plans is the huge new container terminal in the port of Mariel that was built in partnership with Brazil's Odebrecht Group. Just 28 miles (45 km) from Havana, Mariel Bay covers an area of 180 square miles (46,620 hectares) and will operate as a Special Development Zone, offering tax incentives to foreign firms who set up assembly plants, light industry, and warehousing of goods for import into Cuba and for export to Latin America and the US. The contract to run the container port, which opened in 2014 and can accommodate Super-Panamax shipping, was given to PSA International, a port operator from Singapore.

The Cuban government is actively seeking foreign investment and the country organizes several international trade fairs, including the Havana International Fair (FIHAV) in November, and the International Tourism Fair (FITCuba) in May. However, this is not a country where entrepreneurs can simply move in, exploit a gap in the market, and turn a profit. Don't expect a McDonald's on the streets of Havana any time soon—although its trademark is registered in Cuba. This is a country undergoing a cautious and gradual economic transition and the legislation and regulations governing business relationships with

foreign partners can change, and not necessarily predictably. There is no point looking to Cuba for a quick buck—the emphasis is on fairly large businesses doing long-term deals with the Cuban state based on Cuba's requirements and at Cuba's speed. You will need a great deal of patience and willingness to build long-term business relationships.

CUBA AS A BUSINESS PARTNER

Cuba's current preference seems to be for a smaller number of larger projects in strategic sectors, rather than a general opening of its economy in all sectors, but the priorities are changing and new opportunities are opening up, such as medical tourism and the high-tech equipment needed to outfit clinics catering to foreigners. As a business partner, Cuba has advantages over many developing countries, including a well-educated and qualified labor force able to assimilate new technologies rapidly, an adequate or updatable infrastructure, social stability, a generally crime-free environment safe for foreign personnel, and—as throughout its history—a strategic location between the US and Latin America.

Corruption is reassuringly low. Offering sweeteners to officials will not benefit potential investors and could in fact harm their case. Transparency International, which monitors corruption worldwide, placed Cuba 63rd in the world and 6th in Latin America and the Caribbean in its 2014 Corruption Perceptions Index, below Chile and Uruguay but above Peru and Panama.

Last but not least, the US embargo has kept US multinationals and smaller firms out of Cuba, giving non-US firms a competitive advantage in Cuba that they might not have in other Latin American countries.

GOVERNMENT AND BUSINESS

If you do business in Cuba, you will mostly be doing it with the government. The economy is still massively in state hands, the tiny private sector consisting almost entirely of small family businesses that fit into the 201 categories of private enterprise allowed by the state. Foreign companies can set up joint ventures or "mixed enterprises" (*empresas mixtas*) with Cuban government entities. You will need to get to know the precise relationship between the mixed enterprise you are dealing with and the government entities involved.

Profits accruing to the government from any of these enterprises are plowed into social benefits such as subsidized food, transportation, education, and health care. It is important for a business proposal from a foreign entrepreneur to demonstrate tangible benefits to the Cuban people—by creating jobs, paying taxes, and expanding the economy. Entrepreneurs committed to environmental conservation and sustainable development are welcomed.

ProCuba, the Investment Promotion Center of the Ministry for Foreign Investment and Economic Cooperation (MINVEC), keeps a directory of business opportunities and organizes trade events like the Havana International Fair.

THE LEGAL FRAMEWORK

The law in Cuba declares all economic sectors open to foreign investment apart from health care, education, and the armed forces. The legislation emphasizes, however, that any mixed enterprises must contribute to the sustainable social and economic development of the country "on the basis of respect for the country's sovereignty and independence and the protection and rational use of natural resources." Except for some technical and managerial posts, Cuban staff must be hired through the Cuban government employment agency, not directly by the mixed enterprise. There is specific legislation regulating investment in Cuba's free-trade zones and industrial parks and the employment of foreign staff in mixed enterprises.

Investments are authorized by either the Executive Committee of the Council of Ministers or a government commission designated by the Committee, depending on size, proportion of foreign capital involved, and other factors.

Mixed enterprises enjoy some tax reductions: a tax rate of 30 percent is set on profits, and enterprises pay an 11 percent labor force tax and a 14 percent social security contribution. The free-trade zones offer a liberal tax regime with no duties payable on their imports or exports, and assorted tax holidays. There are no restrictions on the repatriation of foreign partners' profits.

THE WORKFORCE

For nearly forty years Cubans were guaranteed jobs for life. However, during the Special Period after 1990, the government laid off many workers in the struggle to stave off financial collapse. Increasing the variety of jobs allowed as self-employment in 2011 was a government response to high unemployment during that period; some have seen the slimming of the civil service as mass redundancy in disguise. Unemployment statistics from Cuba are unavailable, but external sources estimated the unemployment rate in 2013 at 2.5 to 4.1 percent.

Women in Business

The government's legislation and policy have always supported women's waged employment. In 2015 women comprised about 40 percent of the workers in the civilian state sector, in which they represent about 66 percent of all mid- and high-level technicians and professionals. This positive representation of women was reflected in the World Economic Forum's 2014 report on the Global Gender Gap, where Cuba came in 30th place overall and third in Latin America after Nicaragua and Ecuador, with a very similar score to Spain.

Nonetheless, although Cuba is more gender-equal than most Latin American countries, women hold fewer than a third of top managerial positions. Equally, women occupy about 45 percent of the seats in the Cuban parliament but are under-represented at the very top levels of government.

UNIONS

The Cuban concept of trade unions is very different from the norm in Canada, Europe, or the US. The remodeling of the unions after the Revolution presupposed that in a workers' state the interests of the workers and their employer (the government) were identical, so the unions exist to reinforce government policy and ensure that economic aims are met in the interests of the population as a whole, rather than to defend workers against exploitation. The unions also help to meet certain social needs, but their approach is paternalistic.

The Confederation of Cuban Trade Unions, closely connected to the Communist Party, is the only recognized trade union federation. Independent workers' groups within Cuba report that the government does not recognize independent unions, collective bargaining, or the right to strike.

THE IMPORTANCE OF PERSONAL RELATIONSHIPS

A good personal relationship is fundamental to a successful business relationship in Cuba, and it is crucial to have an "opposite number" with whom you get along. It's worth remembering that people have both a social and a personal investment in their business relationships. Establishing a climate of goodwill and trust goes a long way to helping a partnership to proceed smoothly.

Remember, though, that however friendly and enthusiastic your contacts may be, they are operating within a controlled and bureaucratic system fraught with ambiguities. The top echelons of the government want foreign businesses to operate in Cuba to aid the national economy, but are wary of giving away too much state control and concerned about the social inequalities and economic distortions that may arise from increased private enterprise.

BE PREPARED

Cuba may be open for business after decades of isolation from the West, but that does not mean Cuban businesspeople are naive. Official statistics are not always reliable, but misinformation about Cuba is rife, and Cubans will be gratified if you have done some homework and are sensitive to their history and culture.

Thorough preliminary market research into your market niche, partners, and pricing is necessary, and you will need to have established a contact in Cuba before you travel.

Your embassy in Cuba can help with up-to-date information on investing, and imports, and Cuba's MINVEC and others can help you to identify appropriate Cuban counterparts. Bear in mind that as the economy improves, the government is becoming more selective about its partners.

It is important to understand that any business contact must go through official channels. You will not be able to arrange a business meeting without contacting MINVEC, the Economic Counselor at the Cuban embassy in your country, and your country's embassy in Cuba. All these contacts are necessary for you to get a business visa, which is also indispensable. These bodies will also brief you about the business environment in general and opportunities in your particular area.

The best initial access point is participation in a trade mission organized by an appropriate institution. The Chamber of Commerce designs tailor-made itineraries for members of trade missions so they get to meet the relevant people in their area. If you participate in a trade mission, you will always meet the Economic Counselor in the Cuban embassy in your country.

Representatives of government entities at a high enough level to be conducting business discussions will probably be able to communicate well in English, but it will be appreciated—and helpful to you—if you know some Spanish.

MAKING A PROPOSAL

Once a partnership is identified, the next step is to prepare a proposal to be submitted to MINVEC based on a business plan and feasibility study. Your chances of success will be enhanced if you can demonstrate that you have a sound medium-term business strategy and the resources and commitment to carry it out. The proposal must be accompanied by documentation such as legal accreditation of the company proposing the association and its representative, and audited financial statements. A draft goes to MINVEC for its recommendations, and once these are agreed upon the proposal is submitted for authorization.

MEETINGS

Be punctual for meetings. Whatever you may have heard about the Cuban tendency to lateness, you won't create a good impression if you are late. The dress code for business meetings is not formal, but women dress more elaborately than men.

Business meetings can vary in style, and are generally cordial and efficient. The degree of protocol involved depends on the level. If a very high-ranking official is involved, they may make a short presentation or speech. One thing that may surprise foreigners is the number of people who attend: it's not unknown for up to thirty people—practically anyone with a connection to the project being discussed—to come to a meeting, though only two or three will speak. This may look inefficient, but it promotes transparency.

A smaller meeting will probably start with coffee, or even rum, and an ice-breaking chat. Business cards will be exchanged. The meeting may take a long time, allowing plenty of time for the participants to get to know each other. It is pointless to try to speed things up. Be patient.

Cubans are very direct in face-to-face communication, and look squarely at their interlocutors. You should maintain eye contact during a conversation, especially in a formal situation.

If you host a lunch, it should not be too lavish.

NEGOTIATING

Don't expect to be able to draw up a finished contract in one or two visits. Since the level of regulation and centralization is very high, there may not be a great deal of room to maneuver in negotiations. However, there is evidence that greater flexibility is applied in sectors the government is particularly keen to develop, due in part to the chronic shortage of hard currency, and the very limited financing options that Cuba can draw on.

It is important to focus on the individuals who will contribute to a decision on your proposal. The way to influence decisions is not by lobbying them, as is usual in Europe or North America, but by building up a relationship of personal trust—another reason why doing business in Cuba takes time.

DECISION MAKING AND FOLLOW-UP

In state enterprises, decision making almost inevitably involves several levels of government. This is not to say that there won't be a single decision maker at the top who will sign the ultimate authorization (and whose heavy workload may well delay it considerably), but the decision will depend on the gathering and weighing of inputs from many people from ministries and enterprises. How high up the decision goes depends on the size and strategic importance of the project and the divergences of opinion among those who contribute. Although the bureaucracy has lost a lot of weight, it hasn't necessarily become less bureaucratic. Depending on the project, getting from initial approach to approval can take up to twelve months.

At the same time, Cuban enterprises expect replies to their letters, faxes, and telephone calls and may abandon the project if they receive no response. Communications with Cuba are often difficult, but it is vital to keep in touch. Patience and a willingness to keep the relationship—and hence the business—going are fundamental factors.

CONTRACTS

Many aspects of the operation of a mixed enterprise are established at the contract stage, and the clearer and more transparent the contract the better. You will need a lawyer who is familiar with Cuban commercial law. You can find an independent lawyer in Cuba, or go through one of the legal practices in Europe that have offices in Cuba and can provide independent advice. Cubans are more legalistic than most, and won't enter legal agreements that are not clear to them. In this sense, they are closer to North American business culture than to Latin American.

Cases of joint ventures being unilaterally suspended should alert potential investors to the need to make sure all contracts contain clear contingency and compensation clauses covering things such as cost overruns, changes in government policy, or other obstacles to delivery.

RESOLVING DISPUTES

If there is a disagreement over a contract or payment, the first and best option is to try to deal with it straight away. Good local legal advice is essential, as going to court in Cuba over a breach of contract can be a protracted and frustrating process. The best way to avoid disputes is to maintain frequent contact with your business partners, which will help to build strong personal ties and flag up issues before disputes arise. This may mean a closer working relationship than you would expect with a business partner in the USA or UK, and more time spent on the ground.

chapter **nine**

COMMUNICATING

LANGUAGE

Although many Cubans speak English, especially in hotels and resorts, visitors are often surprised by the lack of English on the streets. Pack a phrasebook or dictionary, practice some simple phrases before you go, and you will find a little Spanish gets you a long way when buying things in shops and traveling outside tourist enclaves.

Cubans will appreciate any attempt to speak a few words in their language and if you can produce a *Cubanismo* or two (see opposite) you will certainly get a smile in return. Cuban Spanish is idiosyncratic, peppered with slang, and spoken at great speed, especially in Havana. Cubans also have a tendency to swallow consonants when they speak. Immersing yourself in Cuban songs and learning a few verses of a classic *son cubano* or modern reggaetton is a good way to train your ear to the rhythm of the language before arriving.

The intonation of Cuban Spanish was strongly influenced by Canary islanders, who drop the "s" and swallow the "ado" from the ends of words, and ignore the Spanish lisp on words like *cerveza* (pronouncing it "ser-vay-sah"). Cubans also use the Canarian word *guagua* (bus), instead of the typical Spanish *autobús*. Other words brought from West Africa by slaves, have become popular through Afro–Cuban music and are now in general use. The strong US presence on the island up to 1959 has left a legacy of Cubanized English words like *broder*, *beisbol*, and *frén* (friend), and the glossary of these Spanglish terms continues to expand and evolve.

SPEAK LIKE A CUBAN

Typical Cuban Words

Jaba – a bag

Jama – Food. The verb *jamar* is to to eat. "*Tengo hambre! Vamos a jamar.*" ("I'm hungry! Let's eat.")

Pepe – A foreigner of any nationality

Pincha – A job. The verb *pinchar* is to work. "*Me voy a la pincha.*" ("I'm going to work.")

Yuma – Either *la Yuma*, meaning the US, as in "*Mi primo vive en la Yuma*" ("My cousin lives in the US."), or to describe a visitor from the US, and by extension foreigners, as in "*Oye, Yuma, Ven aca!*" ("Hey, foreigner, come here!"). This Cuban version of the word Gringo is only heard on the island and dates back to the early years of the Revolution when *3:10 to Yuma*, a 1957 Hollywood Western starring Glenn Ford, took on cult status. You will still see murals with defiant anti-imperialist slogans like "Yanqui Go Home," but most Cubans are happy to see *Yumas* on their streets and are hoping more will come.

Cuban Words from Africa
Asére is an Efik word from Nigeria, that is translated as "I salute you" but has come to mean "close friend". It is used in the common greeting: "*Qué bola, asére*?" ("How are you, buddy?")
Chévere, which is used to say something is cool or excellent, also comes from Efik.

Cuban Words from English
Bisnero - Businessman, entrepreneur, or street hustler
Blumer – Panties
Chopin – Referring to a CUC shop. "*Vamos al chopin*!" ("Let's go to a tourist store.")
Chor or chores – shorts
Frigi – Refrigerator (from frigidaire)
Ponchero – Puncture repair man
Pulover – T-shirt
Queik – Cake
Tenis – Sneakers, trainers
Yin – Jeans

WRITTEN COMMUNICATION

The written language is more formal than the spoken language, and indeed can be quite flowery. The general rules for written Spanish apply. As in many other cultures, language in texts and e-mails tends to be less formal and more concise.

As elsewhere in Spanish-speaking countries, Cubans have two surnames, the father's and the mother's. When a woman marries, she adds her husband's name. So Rosalía Pérez López, if she marries Victor Gómez, will sign her name Rosalía Pérez López de Gómez. However, apart from in legal documents, she will still sign her name as Rosalía Pérez López. Her daughter, however, will be Victoria Gómez Pérez. If a Cuban official writes "SOA" on a form by your name, it means "*sin otro apellido*" (no other surname).

FORMS OF ADDRESS

Cubans still often call each other—and sometimes foreigners—*compañero* or *compañera*, the revolutionary form of address introduced after 1959. This is not used at the head of a letter, however, especially with someone you don't know well: use *Señor* (Mr.), *Señora* (Mrs.), or *Señorita* (Miss, usually for a young woman). These can be abbreviated to *Sr.*, *Sra.*, *Srta.* "Dear Sir/Madam" is "*Estimado(a) señor(a)*." When speaking, use *señor, señora, señorita* if you're not sure how to address someone. You can use *compañero* or *compañera* for someone you know better. In any case you will soon be on first-name terms. *Señor(a)* is often used as a mark of respect to older people; you may even hear the old-fashioned *don/doña* (with the person's first name, for example, Don José, Doña Josefina).

In both written and spoken communication, you won't go wrong if you use the formal pronoun *usted* (you) until addressed by the familiar *tú*—but that won't take long, and many Cubans will immediately use *tú*. Once addressed as *tú*, however, don't reply with *usted*—that would come across as a deliberate snub.

DIRECT INTERACTION

Cubans are informal and direct when interacting with other people, and conversations are accompanied by lots of "talking with the hands." People can be very familiar with strangers, cutting right through the formalities and getting straight to the point.

A complete stranger might attract your attention with a loud "*Oye*!" ("Listen! Hey!"), by hissing at you with a "pssst, pssst"—a favorite for attracting the attention of waiters—or by directing a flattering remark your way, such as "*Oye, mi amor*" ("Hey, my love"), or "*Oye, guapo*" ("Hey, handsome"). This is not regarded as impolite in Cuba.

Greetings

There are no iron rules, but—particularly in professional settings—men shake hands with each other, and will usually shake hands with everyone when entering a home or joining a meeting. Between women, a kiss on the cheek is also a standard greeting, even if you don't know the person very well. Cubans are very friendly in their interactions and men might find a handshake is quickly turned into a backslap. This may happen even on first meeting if you have been introduced by a mutual friend. Women, and friends of opposite sexes, tend to greet each other with one or two kisses on the cheek. More kisses will mark your farewells.

Body Language

Cubans are very tactile, and will touch each other to make a point, express support or sympathy, admire an outfit, and so on. You may see two men apparently arguing vehemently, jabbing at each other with a forefinger; it won't be a quarrel, but probably a discussion of the price of shoes or the baseball results. Cubans are very demonstrative and public displays of affection, such as holding hands in the street, kissing, and hugging are typical for courting couples, although it's still rare to see gay men holding hands or kissing in public.

DIMINUTIVE APPRECIATION

Calling people names linked to their physical appearance is usually considered too personal or rude in the United States or Europe but Cubans find it endearing, especially when the diminutive form of the adjective is used by adding "-ito" or "-ita" at the end. Women will hear lines like "*Oye, flaquita*" ("Hey, skinny girl"), whatever their size. A girlfriend will consider it sweet to refer to a chunky boyfriend as "*mi gordito*" ("my little fatty"). Everything depends on the delivery and the tone of voice.

Equally, names are diminutized to add an endearing touch, or for children, so Mariana might be referred to as Marianita, Juan as Juanito.

HUMOR

Quick witted, lighthearted, and irreverent, Cubans tend to respond to hard times and political and economic restrictions with what they call *choteo* (jokes). Cubans love clever puns and giving people and things inventive nicknames, and *choteo* serves as both a commentary on daily life and a safety valve for frustrations.

While making jokes about the nation's leaders might bring problems, there are no restrictions on jokes targeting snail-like bureaucracy, poor transportation, economic woes, the quality and availability of food, and the general contradictions in the Cuban system.

Havana Humor
"Why do Cuban guys cut the "s" off the end of their words? They are saving them up so they can pssst-pssst at all the good-looking girls on the Malecón!"

THE MEDIA

All areas of the media are state-owned, and state-controlled, and follow the government line. The government has never made any secret of its view that the mass media are powerful tools for education, ideological formation, and the development of social consciousness. A foreign editor of *Granma* once said that the role of a revolutionary press is to promote the Revolution, not to criticize it. As on the streets of Cubans town and cities—where apart from revolutionary slogans there are no billboards or neon signs trying to sell you anything—one thing you notice about the state media in Cuba is the absence of advertising.

Television and Radio

There are five TV channels in Cuba. Of these the main ones are Cubavisión and Telerebelde and the more recent Canal Educativo, launched in 2002 as part of the Battle of Ideas. They broadcast a variety of programming, including news bulletins, boxing, baseball, and soccer games, soap operas, old US TV series, and movies. Cultural programming includes music videos, live concerts by Cuban artists, and documentaries about folk music, ballet, and the arts. Of course there are also panel shows and pundits pushing the government line and documentaries denouncing the US embargo and defending the Revolution.

Many hotels also have satellite channels, but in general Cubans do not have access to satellite TV, although some inventive individuals do set up their own satellite dishes, and for others there is access to downloads of US TV programs via "*el paquete semanal*" (see page 159).

There are seven national radio stations. These include Radio Musical Nacional, which specializes in classical music, and Radio Reloj, which has round-the-clock news. Radio Taíno broadcasts Cuban and foreign popular music and information about forthcoming events, eateries, and nightspots. It is the official tourist station and the one to which most radios in public places are tuned.

Many people, especially in and around Havana, tune in to radio stations in southern Florida. In 1985 the exile community in Miami set up Radio Martí to beam anti-socialist and anti-Castro material at Cuba. The Cuban government tirelessly scrambles the signal, not always successfully. The television equivalent, TV Martí, rarely gets past the jamming signal.

Newspapers and Magazines

Granma, the main national newspaper, and the official organ of the Communist Party, is widely read, and street vendors sell out of it very quickly. A weekly version for foreigners, *Granma Internacional*, is published in English, French, German, Portuguese, and Spanish.

Other daily newspapers include *Trabajadores*, representing the trade unions, and *Juventud Rebelde*, the newspaper of the Young Communists' Union (UJC), although all the news in Cuban newspapers follows the same line. There are many provincial newspapers and two weekly business newspapers, *Opciones* and *Negocios en Cuba*. The bilingual cultural weekly *Cartelera* is possibly the most accessible for foreigners.

Magazines include *Bohemia* (cultural and current affairs weekly, founded in 1908), *Prisma* (fortnightly, bilingual, a showcase for revolutionary achievements), *Palante* (humor), and *Revolución y Cultura* and *Gaceta de Cuba* (arts and literature).

Very few international newspapers or magazines are available, although top hotels can provide them. Cubans can access downloads of foreign publications via the informally distributed "*paquete semanal*."

"EL PAQUETE SEMANAL"

Breaking Bad in Cuba? Taylor Swift's latest album? *National Geographic Magazine* widely available? With limited access to the worldwide Web, Cubans have come up with an ingenious solution to feed their desire for information about the world. A kind of offline Internet, it's called "*el paquete semanal*" (the weekly package) and consists of portable hard drives, passed from hand to hand, that contain downloads of the latest Hollywood movies, music, US TV series, documentaries, Latin American soaps, hundreds of magazines, computer games, software, and mobile apps. While a typical *paquete* with a full terabyte of material is expensive, Cubans will pay 1–2 CUC for a portion of it, and then break it down and then swap or sell on a soap opera, movie, or magazine to friends and neighbors. Businesses like *paladres* and beauty salons are now inserting ads into the programs sold in the *paquete*, and new Cuban magazines have been launched in *paquete*-friendly PDF formats. Greater access to Internet will one day make the *paquete* obsolete, but for now it's thriving.

TELEPHONE

Some of Cuba's telecommunications are still based on the pre-1959 system and there can be long delays getting a new landline installed. Although rare nowadays, there are still places where one phone serves the whole village or a block of houses, the owner of the phone going to get whoever has been called, and people lining up outside waiting for pre-arranged calls from relatives abroad. Landlines are sought after because calls are cheaper than from cell phones and calls from a landline to a cell phone are charged to the phone that receives them. In some places it is still not possible to make international calls without going through an operator.

Public pay phones use prepaid magnetic phone cards (*tarjetas telefónicas*) sold in post offices and hotels, and can be used to make direct-dialed international calls. Local, long distance, and international calls can be made (at a price) from hotels or at the Telepunto call centers run by the state telecommunications company ETECSA (Empresa de Telecomunicaciones de Cuba S.A.).

Cell Phones

The cell phone market was opened up to ordinary Cubans in 2008, and by 2015 more Cubans had cell phones than landlines. The main cell phone provider is Cubacel and the 2G mobile network operates on the GSM900 frequency. The majority of android phones and iPhones will work with the Cuban network and there is a thriving market for phones, for those who can afford them (or have relatives abroad who can send an unlocked phone).

Tourists from Canada and Europe can generally use their phones in Cuba, but should check with their network provider. Be aware that roaming charges can be very high and data costs for Internet use exorbitant, although there is usually no charge for receiving texts. One option to reduce costs is to rent a cell phone in Cuba or buy a local SIM card to use in an unlocked phone. The new Wi-Fi hubs can be accessed from your phone with a prepaid scratch card.

USEFUL TELEPHONE NUMBERS
Long-distance call within Cuba from a phone-card public phone **0+ area code**
Long-distance call via operator **00**
Reverse charge international call via operator **09**
Direct-dialed international call from a phone-card public phone **119**
As above, from a hotel **88**
Directory inquiries **113**
Police **116**
Ambulance **114 or 118**
Fire **115**
Operators may not speak English.

INTERNET

Until June 2015 only about 5 percent of Cuban homes had access to the Internet, one of the lowest Internet penetration figures in the world, which is why blogging and social media interaction by Cubans is so rare.

Although large hotels usually have some kind of Internet connection it can be expensive, anything from 4 CUC to 12 CUC an hour, and as slow and frustrating as dial-up was in the 1990s. If your hotel can't oblige, the best place for getting online are the Telepunto call centers run by ETECSA, which has the monopoly over all Internet access in the country. There are Telepuntos in most big cities but out in the countryside it's strictly old school, and you have to make do with a phone call or a postcard if you want to update your friends or family on your status.

There was a new development in June 2015 when ETECSA announced the opening of thirty-five Wi-Fi hotspots across the country using technology provided by the Chinese Telecoms firm Huawei. Anybody with a Wi-Fi enabled smartphone can access the hotspots by buying a prepaid scratch card for 2 CUC an hour. In November 2015 eight more were added, and ETECSA has pledged to open more.

The key to Cuba's Internet expansion has been the ALBA-1 undersea fiber-optic cable connected by Venezuela in 2011, and which only started to take over from satellite traffic in 2015 when it was linked to towns and cities through a backbone of terrestrial connections.

Following US President Obama's reestablishment of diplomatic ties, he issued a special provision that allows telecommunications and information technology business between the two countries. Search engine giant Google has already offered to do business with Cuba, but the government is wary of handing over control of the Internet and instead plans its own C.U.B.A. (Contenidos Unificados para Búsqueda Avanzada) search engine. Ordinary Cubans, meanwhile, want greater access to Skype and Wi-Fi or broadband connections at home.

MAIL

Post offices keep long hours, often 8:00 a.m. to 10:00 p.m., and lines are long on weekends. Stamps and postcards can be bought at large hotels if you want to save time.

The postal service is generally slow, but posting mail at post offices will speed up delivery times. All foreign mail has to pass through Havana, adding a week to items posted in isolated parts of the island. Mail can take ten days to reach North America and three or four weeks to Europe. Cubans often ask travelers to carry mail overseas to post. The safest and fastest way to post urgent mail, parcels, and documents is via an international courier service like DHL, which has offices in all the major cities.

CONCLUSION

Cuba is a country that is easy to enjoy but difficult to decipher for first-time visitors. If you come seeking rum cocktails, hand-rolled cigars, *rumba* dancing, and revolutionary icons, you will not be disappointed. But Cuba can also confound expectations. Those expecting a closed, Communist state will also find Cubans with a wealth of opinions on their country, and its future—and an entrepreneur on every corner, working two, sometimes three, jobs to make ends meet.

The historic reestablishment of diplomatic ties with the US in 2015 augurs well for Cuba's economic future. The partial easing of restrictions under the US embargo has seen an increase in flights and the future prospect of ferry services from the US and cruise ship visits.

However, as we have seen, while many companies are keen to enter the Cuban market, the speed of change will depend entirely on the Cuban government and how much flexibility and freedom it is prepared to allow.

Over the years the Cuban people have suffered many hardships but they remain fiercely proud of their island home, their struggle for independence, their linguistic quirks, and the tropical rhythms that swing Cuban hips.

The Cuban state's emphasis on health, education, sports, and culture is second to none, and a night at the ballet in Havana, surrounded by ordinary Cubans in thrall to the music, movement, and magic of Cuba's world-class performers, is evidence enough of the country's achievements.

As tourism to the island grows and relations with the US gradually thaw, there has never been a better time to visit this unique island and experience its colonial cities, Caribbean beaches, and verdant countryside. With the boom in accommodation options around the island, Cuba is opening up to foreign visitors on a scale not seen before. Cycling, hiking, birdwatching, diving, and fishing adventures are now on the menu alongside sun and sea vacations, culture-focused activity tours, and health tourism.

Whether you travel to Cuba for educational purposes, fun in the sun, or serious business, no trip to the island is ever dull, and it is hard not to be swept up by the passion, ingenuity, and humor of the Cuban people.

Further Reading

History, Politics, Economy
Anderson, Jon Lee. *Che Guevara: A Revolutionary Life*. New York: Grove Press, 2010 (revised ed.).
Castro, Fidel. *My Life. A Biography*. Cambridge and Malden, MA: Polity Press, 2004.
Chomsky, Aviva. *The Cuba Reader*. Durham: Duke University Press, 2004.
Gott, Richard. *Cuba: A New History*. New Haven & London: Yale University Press, 2004.
Guerra Vilaboy, Sergio, and Oscar Loyola Vega. *Cuba: A History*. Melbourne, Australia: Ocean Press, 2014.
Thomas, Hugh. *Cuba: A History*. London: Penguin, 2010.

Travelogues
Ferguson, Ted. *Blue Cuban Nights*. Chichester: Summersdale, 2002.
Hazard, Samuel. *Cuba with Pen & Pencil*. Oxford: Signal Books, 2007.
Murphy, Dervla. *The Island that Dared. Journeys in Cuba*. London: Eland, 2008.
Smith, Stephen. *Cuba: The Land of Miracles*. London: Little Brown Book Group, 2005.

Art, Literature
Acosta, Carlos. *Pig's Foot*. London, New Delhi, New York, Sydney: Bloomsbury, 2013.
Acosta, Carlos. *No Way Home: A Dancer's Journey from the Streets of Havana to the Stages of the World*. New York: Scribner, 2008.
Ades, Dawn. *Art in Latin America*. New Haven & London. Yale University Press, 1989.
Blair, Peggy. *Midnight in Havana*. Edinburgh: Polygon, 2013.
Greene Graham. *Our Man in Havana*. London: Penguin Classics, 2007.
Padura, Leon. *Havana Fever*. London: Bitter Lemon Press, 2009.

Language
Spanish. A Complete Course. New York: Living Language, 2005.
In-Flight Spanish. New York: Living Language, 2001.
Fodor's Spanish for Travelers (CD Package). New York: Living Language, 2005.

Index

Abakuá cult 57, 67
abortion 58
accommodation 132–4
Afro-Cuban religion (Santería; Rule of Ochá) 10, 55, 56–7, 65–7, 92
air travel 122–3
art galleries 107, 113
arts, the 107–114
  censorship 114
  cinema and theater 111–13
  literature and books 113–14
  music and dance 108–111
  visual arts 113

banks 27
Baracoa 12, 18, 19, 84
Batista, Fulgencio 16, 27–8, 29, 31, 43, 70, 119
bicycles 49, 86, 120, 131–2
body language 154–5
bureaucracy 36, 45, 50, 53, 85, 148
buses 70, 85, 125–6, 131
business briefing 138–49
  be prepared 145–6
  contracts 149
  Cuba as a business partner 140
  decision making and follow-up 148
  the economic climate 138–40
  government and business 141
  the legal framework 141–2
  making a proposal 146
  meetings 146–7
  negotiating 147–8
  personal relationships 144
  resolving disputes 149
  unions 143–4
  the workforce 142–3
business cards 147

calendar
  Catholic 62–4
  political and historical 67–8
Camagüey 10, 73, 124
campsites 134
car rental 127–8
carnivals 70–73
cars 8, 49, 86, 122, 127
casas particulares (guesthouses) 17, 45, 50, 84, 133, 136
Castro, Fidel (main references) 27–33, 35–42
Castro, Raúl 8, 9, 17, 26, 30, 31, 39–43, 47, 59
Catholic Church 17, 39, 55–6
Catholicism 10, 55–6
  traditions 62–4
Cayo Coco 79, 83, 133
Cayo Guillermo 133
Cayo Santa Maria 79
cell phones 160
censorship 43, 114
character 8, 9, 49, 76, 86, 164
child care 58
choteo (lighthearted humor) 48, 80, 155
Christmas Day 63, 70
Ciego de Ávila 73
cigars 116–17
cinema 111–12
cities 10, 117–18
  travel in 130–32
climate 10, 14–16
clothing 79–80
clubs 28, 55, 132
cocktails 106–7
collectivization 89
Columbus, Christopher 17, 18
Committees for the Defense of the Revolution (CDRs) 99
community spirit 52
community-based activities 98
constitution 28, 34, 39, 55
contracts 149
conversations 80–83, 154
cooperation 52
corruption 27, 140
credit cards 103
crime and safety 136–7
Cubania 48–9
cultural festivals 68–9
currency 11, 86–7, 116, 103
cycling 120

daily life 96–7
dance 48, 57, 62, 71, 85, 100, 110–111
decision making and follow-up 148
diminutives 155
disability 94
disputes, resolving 149
dissent 43, 52–3
divorce 58
drinks 105–7
driving
  car rental 127–8
  rules of the road 128–9
drugs 136, 137

eating out 78
economy 16, 32–3, 38, 43–5, 138–40, 141
education 9, 42, 46, 50, 54, 61, 87, 89, 94–5, 164
emigration 16, 38, 96
entrepreneurs 45, 141
ethnic makeup 10, 54
Evangelicals 10
expat groups 84
eye contact 77, 147

family 95–6
farmers markets 38, 101
ferries 129, 163
fifteenth birthday celebrations (girls) 74–5
fishing 120
food 101–5
foreigners, attitudes toward 60–61
forms of address 153

GDP per capita 11
geography 12–14
gifts 78
government 10, 40–1
 and business 141
greetings 154
Guantánamo 12, 26
Guevara, "Che" (Ernesto) 29, 30, 31, 32, 42, 51, 67, 68

Hatuey 19
Havana (La Habana) 8, 10, 12, 14, 15, 20, 21, 56, 60, 64, 70, 72, 84, 117–18, 123, 136–7
health 44, 134–6, 164
health care 9, 42, 46, 50, 54, 61, 87, 89, 92–3, 94, 96, 134–5
heroes and symbols 51
history 16–39
 origins and conquest 17–19
 plunder and piracy 20
 brief British occupation 21
 sugar rush 21–2
 three wars of independence from Spain 23, 25
 the pseudo-republic 25
 the big US sugar boom 26–7
 rise of Batista 27–8
 from Moncada to the Sierra Maestra 28–31
 revolution 31
 the empire strikes back 31–2
 economic reform 32–3
 the Bay of Pigs 16, 68, 133
 the missile crisis 8, 16, 133–4
 in the Soviet fold 134–5
 La Rectification 135–6
 Soviet collapse and the Special Period 16, 36–7
 exile the Cuban way 37–8
 tourism takes over and Fidel steps down 38–9
hitchhiking 128
HIV/AIDS 93–4
Holguin 10, 18
homosexuality 38, 58–9, 155
hospitality 78
hotels 38, 84, 103, 129, 132–3, 135, 136
housing 90–91
humor 80, 155–6, 164
hurricanes 15–16

insects 136
Internet 11, 161–2
investment 38, 133, 139, 142
Isle of Youth (Isla de la Juventud) 12, 14, 68

Jehovah's Witnesses 10, 55
Jews 10, 56
jineteros/as (street hustlers) 76–7, 82, 136

kissing 154, 155

language 10, 85, 150–52
law in Cuba 137, 141–2
libreta (ration book) 88
life expectancy 86, 87
literacy 33, 86, 87, 98
literature and books 113–14

machismo 57, 58
magazines 11, 158
mail 162–3
making friends 76–85
 breaking out of the tourist bubble 83–5
 conversations 80–83
 meeting people 77–9
 staying longer 85
 what to wear 79–80
marriage 82, 96
Martí, José 24, 25, 29, 37, 42, 48, 51, 68, 95
Matanzas 125
media 11, 156–9
medical tourism 44, 134, 164
meeting people 77–9
meetings (business) 146–7
mental health 94
"mixed enterprises" 141–2
motorcycles 131, 132
multiracial Cuba 54–5
museums 83, 107, 119
music 48, 62, 67, 85, 100, 107, 108–110, 164
Muslims 56

national parks 14, 121
negotiating 147–8
New Year's Day 70
newspapers 11, 157–8

Obama, Barack 8, 17, 26, 32, 44, 47, 83
orishas (gods) 57, 65, 66
outdoor activities 115–16

paladares (small restaurants) 17, 47, 50, 85, 102, 103, 105, 136, 159
Palo Monte (Rule of Mayombé) 67

paquete semanal, el (the weekly package) 61, 157, 158, 159
patriotism 50–51
pharmacies 135
photography 137
Pinar del Rio 12, 15, 73
piropos (chat-up lines) 82–3
police 129, 137
political system 39–43
  human rights situation 39, 42–3
  mass organizations 41–2
  the one-party state 10, 37, 39–40
  parliament and elections 40–41
  tropical socialism? 42
population 10, 13, 14, 96
pornography 137
private enterprise 35, 42, 45–6, 50, 52, 101, 144
private houses, accommodation in 17, 45, 50, 84
proposal, business 146
prostitution 58
Protestants 10, 55
public holidays 70, 71
punctuality 78–9

Quakers 10
quality of life 86–8

race, attitudes toward 54–5
radio 11, 157
railways 122, 123–5
rationing 8, 9, 16, 46, 87, 88, 101
religion 10, 43, 55–7
Remedios 73
remittances 44, 46, 54–5, 74
resilience and resourcefulness 49–50
restaurants 17, 45, 50, 102–3, 136
revolutionary Cuba 119
road rules 128–9
"rural urbanization" 89

saints' days 64
Santa Clara 31, 119, 124
Santiago de Cuba 10, 15, 28, 72–3, 118, 124
self-employment 38, 45, 138, 142
senior citizens 96
sexual life 57–8, 81–2, 137
shaking hands 76, 154
shopping 84, 116
Siboney people 17, 18–19
slavery 16, 20, 21, 22, 23, 24, 56, 58, 65, 70
smoking 136
sports 100, 114–15, 164
surnames 152–3

Taíno people 17, 18–19, 54
taxation 142
taxis 122, 127, 130
telephone 11, 27, 159–61
television 11, 61, 156–7
theater 112–13
tipping 102
toilets 135
tourism 8–9, 16, 38, 44, 54, 60, 73, 74, 83, 86–7, 115, 133, 136, 137, 138
tourist cards 84
tours 83, 85
town and country 88–90
trade 17, 20, 21, 22
trade embargo, US 8, 16, 26, 32, 39, 43, 47, 94, 138–9, 140, 163
Trinidad 10, 64, 119
trucks 126

unemployment 138, 142
unions 143–4
"urban ruralization" 90
utilities 87, 89

vaccination 134
Varadero 73, 83, 123, 133
Velázquez de Cuéllar, Diego 17–18
Virgin of Charity of El Cobre 56, 63, 64–5
visas 38, 53
visual arts 113
volunteer work 85, 98

wages 87
waterbuses (*lanchas*) 131
weddings 73–4
wildlife 120–21
women 68
  in business 143
workforce 138, 142–3
written communication 152–3

Acknowledgments

This book would not have been possible without Mandy Macdonald's first edition and the tremendous work she undertook to compile such a broad and balanced account of Cuba. I must also acknowledge the extremely valuable contribution of many Cuban friends, both in Cuba and abroad, who shared with me their stories of daily life on the island. The Cuba Tourist Board, UK, were also very helpful. As always, Francisco de Jesus has been my inspiration, and Alfred Maddicks has been a steadfast support.